P9-DNQ-486

R.D. Bartlett and Patricia P. Bartlett

Corn Snakes and Other Rat Snakes

With 65 Color Photographs

and 14 Range Maps

Illustrations by Michele Earle-Bridges

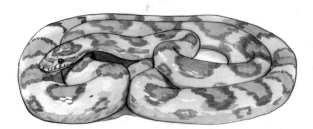

BARRON'S

© Copyright 1996 by Barron's Educational Series, Inc.

All rights reserved.

No part of this book may be reproduced in any form by photostat, microfilm, xerography, or any other means, or incorporated into any information retrieval system, electronic or mechanical, without the written permission of the copyright owner.

All inquiries should be addressed to:
Barron's Educational Series, Inc.
250 Wireless Boulevard
Hauppauge, NY 11788

International Standard Book No. 0-8120-9622-3

Library of Congress Catalog Card No. 95-50351

Library of Congress Cataloging-in-Publication Data
Bartlett, Richard D., 1938–
    Corn snakes and other rat snakes / R.D. Bartlett and Patricia P. Bartlett ; illustrations by Michele Earle-Bridges.
        p. cm.—(A complete pet owner's manual)
    Includes bibliographical references (p. 101) and index.
    ISBN 0-8120-9622-3
    1. Rat snakes as pets. I. Bartlett, Patricia Pope, 1949– II. Title. III. Series.
SF459.S5B37   1996
639.3'96—dc20   95-50351
                                                      CIP

Printed in Hong Kong

9876543

About the Authors

R.D. Bartlett is a herpetologist who has authored more than 400 articles and three books, and coauthored an additional six books. He lectures extensively and has participated in field studies across North and Latin America. In 1970 he began the Reptilian Breeding and Research Institute, a private facility. Since its inception, more than 200 species of reptiles and amphibians have been bred at the RBRI, some for the first time in the United States under captive conditions. Successes at the RBRI include several endangered species.

Bartlett is a member of numerous herpetological and conservation organizations, a co-host on an "on-line" reptile and amphibian forum, and a contributing editor of *Reptiles* magazine.

Patricia Bartlett is a biologist and historian who has authored five books and coauthored six books. A museum administrator for the last 15 years, she has worked in both history and science museums. She received the American Public Works Association Heritage Award in 1985 and serves in numerous local and state organizations.

Photo Credits

All photos by R.D. Bartlett except for the following: photos on pages 48 and 55 by Bill Love of Glades Herp; on pages 39 (top and bottom) and 66 by Ernie Wagner.

Cover Photos

Front: yellow rat snake (*E. obsoleta*); inside front: red-tailed green rat snake (*gonyosoma oxycephalum*); inside back: corn snake (*E. g. guttata*); back: leopard rat snake (*E. situla*).

Contents

The cloudy eyes of this corn snake indicate an impending skin-shedding. Normally "tame" rat snakes may be hostile when their vision is so impaired.

Acknowledgments

As there is in any compilation of notes and materials, when a book such as this is written, personal input from others in the field is sought. Such was the case here. Bill Love and Rob MacInnes of Glades Herp, and Chris McQuade of Gulf Coast Reptiles (both of Ft. Myers, Florida) unhesitatingly provided both slides and photographic opportunities. Eric Thiss (Excelsior, Minnesota), Bill Brant and Joe Hiduke of The Gourmet Rodent and Bruce Morgan (all of Gainesville, Florida) also allowed us to photograph many specimens. Richard Funk, D.V.M., provided medication charts and information. Jim Harding offered thoughts regarding fox snakes in Michigan, and Carl May shared his findings on anerythristic corn snakes in southern Florida. Information and thoughts on natural history and captive care were offered by Mike Souza (green rat snake), Bruce Morgan (various species), Chris Newman (Moellendorff's rat snake), and Ernie Wagner (European rat snakes). Additionally, Ernie Wagner offered slides and, when evaluating our manuscript, enhancements. And, lastly, but certainly not "leastly," our editor at Barron's, Mary Falcon, offered suggestions and support throughout this project. To all, our most sincere thanks.

Preface

It is nice for those of us with herpetological inclinations to know that a good-sized snake can continue to hold its own amid the concrete jungles built by humans. It can. It has.

Thirty years ago, when Miami was a sleepy little town, the author used to see corn and Everglades rat snakes almost daily. Then Miami grew and he moved elsewhere, seldom even visiting the city. Last year, he returned in an attempt to determine the status of the introduced lizard known as the rainbow whiptail. Turning rocks that lay against a warehouse in the downtown area, he found not a whiptail (although they were all around), but a pretty, half-grown corn snake. It was fat and healthy in appearance and gave no indication of being any more stressed by this urban habitat than one of its congeners would have been in the rural vastness of north Florida. The lesson here is that rat snakes (at least some of them) are adaptable, and can coexist peacefully with humans.

Rat snakes in general, and corn snakes in particular, have become the mainstays of an increasingly herp-oriented pet industry. In the cadre of dedicated herpeticulturists who have refined breeding techniques, this upsurge in serpentine popularity is not detrimental to wild populations. While a few corn snakes are still collected from the wild, most of the tens of thousands that are sold annually are babies that have been captive-bred.

Not only *are* corn snakes captive-bred, but selective breeding has yielded albinos and melanistics, as well as corns with redder reds and paler pales. The captive breeding of rat (and king) snakes is now a business that yields many millions of dollars in annual sales.

Often the very first snake of budding enthusiasts, that first corn snake starts an ever-widening circle of interests. Herpetoculture, herpetology, and conservation are all closely tied, and all are tremendously relevant to our interests. Branching out from rat snakes found in the United States to Latin America, Europe, and Asia as well, we discovered that all "rat snakes" aren't necessarily *rat* snakes, and not all are possessed of benevolent dispositions.

In this book, we have tried to offer you an overview of the available rat snake species from the United States, Europe, and, to a lesser extent, Asia. Some of the experiences recounted were Dick's alone, and occurred before we met. Some of them happened since then (and sometimes we remember events differently). We hope that our comments on these pages will help you develop a greater interest in rat snakes and other herptiles, and will assist you in providing the best of conditions for those in your care.

Dick and Patti Bartlett

About Rat Snakes

What Is a Rat Snake?

Compared to the lizards, from which they evolved, snakes are evolutionary newcomers. As best we know, snakes first appeared during the Cretaceous period about 140 million years ago. The serpentine form seems to have been efficient. Certainly, extreme attenuation and narrow girth allow easy access to small areas. There are also legless lizards and serpentine fish such as eels.

In the strictest sense, rat snakes are terrestrial and arboreal species of colubrine snakes from North and Central America, Europe, and Asia. As we have defined rat snakes in this book, we can add South America and North Africa to the range.

The Basics

Most rat snakes look something like a loaf of bread in cross-section—rounded on the top, flat(ish) on the lower sides, and flat on the bottom. The belly scales (or *scutes*) are angled at both sides, which helps in climbing. The scaly skin is dry to the touch. In fact, the scales are *formed* of intricately folded areas of skin. Rat snakes have no remnants of external limbs or pelvic girdle.

The Senses

• The "ear" is wholly internal, and consists of a single earbone that is attached to a jawbone rather than a tympanum. Snakes can hear low frequency sounds well and they react to ground vibrations with alacrity.
• The eye is protected by a *brille*, a single transparent scale. Snake vision ranges from poor to acute, with the rat snakes being on the higher end of this scale. Motion, either by predators or prey, is readily perceived.
• Both ground and airborne molecules of scent adhere to the extended tongue that brings the molecules into contact with the sensory Jacobson's organ (see Glossary, page 100) in the palate. Analysis of the molecules is remarkably acute. Pheromones indicating reproductive readiness and the odors of food animals are only two of the items regularly discerned.

Breathing

Only the right lung is fully functional. Thus, with only a single working lung, respiratory problems are especially serious.

Movement

The forward movement of the rat snake is accomplished by a side-to-side "serpentine movement." Irregularities in the substrate provide traction for the muscular, wavelike, side-to-side motions. The smoother the surface, the harder it is for the snake to crawl across it.

Reproduction

Rat snakes lay eggs (the sole exception being the questionably classified *Elaphe rufodorsata*, see page 88). Depending on the type, some cooler types hatch after about two weeks; others from warmer climes may take more than 60 days. Fertilization is internal, the male accomplishing intromission with either one of the two hemipenes.

Understanding Rat Snakes

The term "rat snake" is used generically to describe unrelated snakes that feed on rats. However, when used by Americans and Europeans, the term refers to rat-eating constrictors of the genus *Elaphe* (EE-LAFF-FEE) and a few closely related genera. They are fairly easy to find. Within the ranges of these snakes, wherever rodents congregate, you are apt to find the predatory rat snakes. This is not to say that occasional specimens will not readily consume baby chicks (or occasionally eggs) if available, but they are largely enthusiastic predators of rats.

Behavior: Despite being robust and powerful, these snakes are also secretive, and most species are especially so by day. They are most apt to be active in the late afternoon, at dusk, and for an hour or two after nightfall. Occasionally, they may wander widely on overcast days.

Taxonomy: Until rather recently the rat snakes of the Americas were placed in a single genus, *Elaphe;* however, with new research, and a changing attitude toward taxonomy, the American rat snakes are now split into three genera: *Elaphe*, the typical rat snakes (including the corn, black, and Baird's rat snakes); *Bogertophis*, the Trans-Pecos and Baja California rat snakes; and *Senticolis*, the green rat snakes.

Availability: Until recently, snake-keeping was a hobby for comparatively few people. Today, snakes are very much a mainstream "pet," and are becoming more so with every passing year. While it is true that many species

of snakes are available, only a few are available in almost inexhaustible supply. These are the species that are now captive-bred by hobbyists and commercial breeders, including several of the American rat snakes. Foremost is the beautiful creature called *corn snake* by some and *red rat snake* by others. (We'll use the name *corn snake* since this is the standardized common name.)

What Is Covered in this Book?

This book covers rat snakes commonly available in the pet market. We have made no effort to discuss many of the seldom seen Asian taxa here. Even so, you will note that the lion's share of this coverage has been directed at the many morphs, normal and selectively derived, of the American corn and black rat snake complexes that, together, are probably the most commonly kept and extensively bred of the world's snake species. Although a basic text, we hope that the comments made here will benefit both neophyte and experienced keepers.

New versus Old World

Strangely, among the rat snakes of the world, the American rat snakes are also among the easiest to keep and breed. Both of these factors have contributed to their ready availability and inexpensive prices. Conversely, although we do not yet know exactly why, many of the Old World rat snakes are difficult to keep, not to mention breed. When Old World species are available, either from the wild or as captive-born hatchlings from the small cadre of hobbyists to have succeeded with them, the prices are high. The compensation for the high prices is that the captive-bred and hatched specimens of many "difficult species" seem considerably easier to maintain than wild collected specimens.

Our tip: With this in mind, we suggest that before purchasing a rat snake you ask to see it feed (if you are purchasing it locally from a breeder-hobbyist or pet shop), or get explicit assurance from the supplier that the snake is feeding.

Rat Snake Colors and Patterns

Throughout the world, the patterns and colors of rat snakes repeat themselves over and over. The hatchlings and juveniles of many are prominently blotched and, as growth occurs, the blotches fade and may be replaced by longitudinal striping. Many widely separated species are remarkably similar in external appearance; for example, the pretty saddled pattern of the American corn snake, *Elaphe g. gutatta*, is echoed in the European leopard snake, *E. situla*, as well as in the Latin American *E. flavirufa*, and the Transcaucasian rat snake, *E. hohenackeri*, and, to a lesser degree, in the Chinese red-headed rat snake, *E. moellendorfi*. The striping of several of the European rat snakes (*E. quatuorlineata* and *E. scalaris* among them) is quite reminiscent of the striping seen on the American yellow rat snake, *E. obsoleta quadrivittata* and the Japanese *E. quadrivirgata*.

Defenses/Offenses

Teeth on one end: Everyone knows that snakes bite. Even the most innocuous of the nonvenomous species can and will bite if threatened. Rat snakes are certainly no exception

and, even those captive-bred and hatched for many generations will occasionally bite.

All rat snakes have teeth. Those of rat snakes are small, in several rows (four in the upper jaw, two in the lower) and have a recurved structure, which is designed to prevent the escape of prey items once grasped. Snakes don't chew their food; they overpower it and swallow it whole.

If you are bitten, don't jerk away as the snake will be unable to disengage its teeth quickly enough to prevent tearing your skin. Your jerking may actually pull the snake's teeth out of its jaw. Give the snake a moment to disengage its teeth, then move away.

You will soon learn the best method of avoiding injury is to avoid bites. It won't take a great amount of observation on your part to determine when and whether your rat snake is upset. If it is, either leave it alone or handle the snake carefully with a snake hook.

If you are bitten, remove any teeth that may remain in the wound, wash the bite carefully, and administer an antiseptic/antibacterial agent. A bandage will remind you to be more careful and elicit sympathy from your friends—unless they keep snakes as well.

Besides biting, how do rat snakes protect themselves?

Muscles in the middle: If restrained (especially near the head or neck) the snake will coil tightly around the restraining object and try to pull free. The amount of strength possessed by the snake is remarkable.

Musk at the other end: Also if restrained, rat snakes will musk, and smear the contents of the anal glands and intestinal tract on their captor. This is odoriferous and disconcerting, but not of serious consequence. Although this admonition is probably entirely unnecessary, wash carefully if smeared.

The Ethics and Arguments Regarding Hybridization

As long as simple intergrades and hybrids are produced solely for the pet trade, we see nothing at all wrong with such breeding programs.

When the practice was first begun by herpetoculturists, it was deplored by conservationists and herpetocultural purists alike. Understandably, these two groups remain opposed to the practice. Much of the antihybridization furor was brought on by the breeders themselves who claimed breeding as a conservation/reintroduction tool.

Intergrades and/or hybrids should *never* be released into the wild, no matter how depleted wild stocks actually do become; thus, neither intergrades nor hybrids could ever be anything but pet trade specimens. The only conservation value from them is that their availability may reduce pet trade collecting of wild specimens.

It would have been more acceptable if the hobbyists (the vast majority of whom will *never* be involved with any serious conservation program) had simply said "We are now producing serpentine 'mutts' for the pet industry. This effort is a money-maker for us, and the conservation aspects, if any, are simply that purchasers of our snakes will not be drawing as heavily on wild populations and will, hopefully, be learning respect for a beleaguered group of animals." The conservationists and purists would still have been alarmed, but one argument against the practice would have been largely defused.

So, if we don't breed snakes for conservation, why *do* we breed them? Because we want to, because we

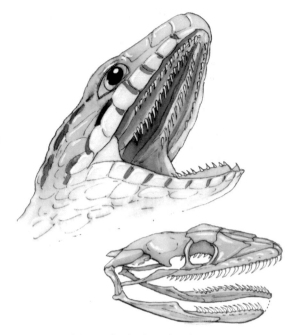

No wonder it hurts. Snake jaw, showing multiple rows of teeth.

enjoy them, because we can learn from them! Certainly these are reasons enough.

An additional conservation note: Remember, as we have said, genetically manipulated snakes should *never* be released. Humans are doing enough to compromise the efforts of Mother Nature without throwing another variable into the melting pot. Genetic purity must be retained in the wild and it is up to us, as more than casually interested parties, to assure that it is—or that at least our efforts and mistakes do not contribute to its degradation.

Acquiring Your Rat Snake

Choosing a Healthy Rat Snake

Keeping a rat snake in captivity over a long period of time is a lot easier if you start with a healthy snake. Actually determining the state of health of a potential purchase may be somewhat difficult to do, because, like all reptiles, rat snakes may behave normally—show no outward signs of ill health—until they are seriously ill. But there are a few clues to look for when choosing a pet rat snake, or a snake of any species.

An arboreal rat snake lies quietly in a tree fork.

Basic behavior. This is one clue. Rat snakes are often secretive, surviving by staying out of the way of possible predators, and remaining beneath cover for long periods. Rat snakes tend to be "wait-and-ambush" predators; they simply wait until prey happens along in front of them. Arboreal types may remain quietly sprawled along a sturdy limb or leaning trunk. This quiet demeanor may make them seem less than alert, but actually nothing could be further from the truth.

Ask an expert. Until you become entirely familiar with rat snakes and their normal behavior, take a knowledgeable person with you when you go to pick one out. Select a snake that displays an alert demeanor when disturbed. Keep in mind that some species are naturally more belligerent than others. Corn snakes, for example, are fairly calm rat snakes. This is where knowledge and experience—if not your own, then someone else's—will come in handy. In addition to looking for a calm snake, if you're a beginner, choose one of the hardier types of rat snakes.

Does it eat? When choosing your snake, look at its general appearance. Check the overall size and body weight. Although some species are normally more slender than others, a lengthwise skin fold along the sides or "accordion" ribs is a caution sign. Fattening up a rat snake may not be possible. Ask the dealer, private or commercial, about the snake. Ask if the specimen is feeding and watch it feed, if possible.

Sneezing. Ask if the snake is sneezing. A snake that is sneezing may have a respiratory infection; labored breathing may mean that lung flukes are present. Both of these problems are hard to diagnose in a living snake and postmortem diagnosis is frustrating for you and pointless for that snake.

Will it bite? Ask if the snake can be handled. A snake that does not strike wildly at an approaching hand will be easier for you to take care of once you get it home.

If given good care, many rat snakes are wonderful and often long-lived snakes. It is not unusual for a rat snake of any type to live upwards of ten years in captivity. If you choose your specimen(s) carefully, the chances are good that you will become a satisfied hobbyist.

Handling: Do's and Don'ts

Use a hook. Although many rat snakes do not object to gentle handling, others may never adjust to it. This is especially true of many of the Asian rat snake species, some of which not only wriggle wildly when held, but bite indiscriminately. Consider these snakes display animals only—animals to be watched and appreciated, lifted, moved, and manipulated on a snake hook, but not handled.

Use a box. Add a cardboard or plastic hiding box to the cage. Many specimens will remain quietly in their hidebox. If the hidebox has a secure bottom, hidebox and all can be lifted and moved without disturbing the snake.

Be gentle. When you do hold a rat snake, remember that even a rather small specimen can and will bite a hand painfully hard if the snake is carelessly restrained. Even such relatively easy-to-handle specimens as corn snakes and yellow rat snakes do not like to be suddenly grasped. Handle all

specimens gently; do not tap on the terrarium glass or cage front, and, if your specimen displays reluctance at being lifted, manipulate it first with a hook.

Even if your snake bites you, do not drop it. A drop can result in damage to internal organs or broken bones. Although arboreal species may be a little more accustomed to an occasional fall, they still should never be handled carelessly.

Location Matters

The hobby of keeping reptiles is, of course, not limited to any one section of the United States, Europe, or Asia; however, the availability of reptiles is, unquestionably, better in some regions of those countries than in others.

Dealers

In the United States, the largest reptile dealers are located in California, Florida, and New York. Reptiles are shipped by air freight from the larger cities in these states to wholesalers in other cities who, in turn, supply pet shops and, in some cases,

Use a hook to move species that do not adjust to handling.

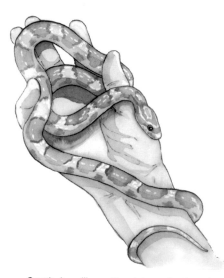

Gentle handling will quiet most rat snakes species.

dealers. Specialty dealers may breed reptiles themselves and also deal directly with other breeders, world-wide; they are often better able to answer your questions. Their imported specimens are usually acclimated, have been fed, and have often been subjected to a veterinary checkup. It is from the specialty dealers that the broadest selection of the world's rat snakes are usually available.

Breeders

Breeders, whether specialist hobby-ists or commercial breeders, are prob-ably the best sources of parasite-free, well-acclimated specimens and accu-rate information. Most breeders keep records of genetics, lineage, fecundity, health, and the quirks of the speci-mens with which they work. These records are invariably available to their customers.

This isn't what I ordered! Keep in mind that most rat snake species change color and/or pattern (some dra-matically so) throughout their long lives. Some are blotched and pale as babies, and striped and richly colored as adults; others may just be paler diminutives of the adults. While a breeder or dealer may well know what the adult breeder rat snakes look like, it is impossible to guarantee that the offspring will be identical. After all, you don't look exactly like your parents. Reputable dealers and breeders will do anything possible to provide you with the finest quality stock, but, despite all your purveyor's efforts, at adulthood your snake may end up being duller or brighter than its parents—or even very like them. Be prepared for all eventualities.

Shipping, if Necessary

There is a good chance that the specimen(s) you seek will be available only from a dealer or breeder at some distance from you. In this case, you'll need to have the rat snakes shipped to

herpetocultural breeders. There is usually some overlap among these businesses.

Pet Stores

Although most pet shops can pro-vide good information on the animals they sell, some rely on information given to them by their distributors/sup-pliers. Unfortunately, information given, even inaccurate information, is often self-perpetuating.

There are some facts that your shop cannot reasonably be expected to know. Among these are the origin of a given wild-collected specimen and the genetics of either normal-appear-ing or aberrant specimens that are captive-bred. Remember, your local pet shop is often two or even three or four times removed from the source of the specimen.

Specialty Dealers

The continuing growth in popularity of reptiles has created the specialty

you by air. For a hobbyist who has not done this before, shipping may seem intimidating. Be assured that the chances are excellent that your supplier is quite familiar with shipping and will be delighted to assist you in any way possible.

There are many things that must be considered when air transportation is involved, among them being the method of payment to be used, the best time to ship, where you should have your shipment sent, and what the best airline is to use. Let's explore some of your choices.

Payment

This should be agreed upon, and fully understood at the time of ordering, but bear in mind that you generally pay for the animal and the shipping charges in advance. It will probably be necessary to get a money order or cashier's check to the shipper, or to supply the shipper with a credit card number, or wire transfer of funds to his/her account. Many shippers will accept personal checks but will not ship until the check has cleared their bank (usually within a week or so).

An alternate method of payment is C.O.D.; however, this can be expensive and inconvenient. Most airlines will accept cash only for the C.O.D. amount and there is a hefty collection fee (upwards of $15.00) in addition to all other charges.

Shipping by Air
• Give your supplier your full name, address, and current day *and* night telephone numbers where you can be reached.
• Inform your shipper of the airport you wish to use, or agree on a door-to-door delivery company. If your area is serviced by more than one airport (such as the Washington D.C. or San Francisco areas), be very specific about the airport.

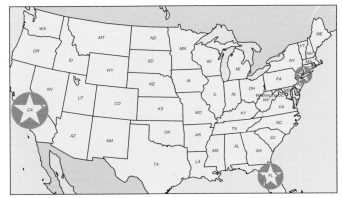

If you want to buy directly from a dealer, look towards New York, California, or Florida.

• Agree on a date and get the airbill number from the supplier. Avoid weekend arrivals when the cargo offices at most small airports are closed. Some shippers go to the airport on one or two specific days each week. Work out a shipping date in advance. Allow enough time for your shipment to get to you before panicking. Most shipments take about 24 hours to get from the airport of origin to the airport of destination. It may take less time if you are lucky enough to be served by direct flights; it may take more time if you're in an area with limited flights and the shipment has to be transferred one, two, or more times.
• Keep your shipment on the same airline whenever possible; with live animals you pay for each airline involved.
• Ship *only* during good weather. Your snake may be delayed when the weather is very hot, very cold, or during the peak holiday travel/shipping/mailing times.
• Most airlines offer three choices: regular "space available" freight (the most frequently used and the suggested service level), air express (guaranteed flights), or small package (the fastest level of service). You will pay premium

Open the shipping crate and inspect your purchases.

prices for either of the last two levels but they may be required by the air line if shipping conditions are adverse. Compare airlines. Some carriers charge a lot more than others for the same level of service.

Arrival of Your Shipment

After a reasonable time, call the airline on which your shipment is traveling and ask them for the status of the shipment. The airline will need the airbill number to trace the shipment in their computer.

Pick your shipment up as quickly after its arrival as possible. This is especially important in bad weather. Learn the hours of your cargo office and whether the shipment can be picked up at the ticket counter if it arrives after the cargo office has closed.

You will have to pay for your shipment (including all C.O.D. charges and fees) before you can inspect it. Once you are given your shipment, open and inspect it *before* leaving the cargo facility.

If there's a problem: Unless otherwise specified, reliable shippers guarantee live delivery; however, to substantiate the existence of a problem, both shippers and airlines will require a discrepancy or damage report made out, signed, and dated by airline personnel. In the very rare case when there is a problem, insist on the filling out and filing of a claim form right away and contact your shipper *immediately* for instructions.

After the first time, you will no longer find the shipping of specimens onerous—Understanding the system will open wide new doors of acquisition.

Your Rat Snake's Health

Shedding

The age and health of your rat snake will have much to do with the frequency with which it sheds its skin. A healthy, fast-growing baby will shed its skin several times a year, much more frequently than a slowly growing adult or an ill specimen. A specimen suffering from a mite infestation or from a malady known as blister disease (see page 19), however, will usually enter a rapid shed cycle no matter what the snake's age is. If the irritation factor is corrected (the mites eliminated or the cage cleaned and dried), all evidence of the disease will often disappear after two or three sheds.

Adult rat snakes will shed their skin soon after emerging from hibernation (or brumation—the terms are basically interchangeable). Following this springtime shed, most rat snakes have cycled or are cycling for breeding. Females shed again prior to egg deposition.

The shedding process (also called molting, or, more properly, *ecdysis*) results from thyroid activity. A week or so prior to shedding, as the old skin begins to loosen from the new one forming beneath it, your rat snake's skin may dull and take on an overall grayish or silvery sheen. The snake's eyes will temporarily look bluish. A snake in this phase is colloquially referred to as *blue* or *opaque* by hobbyists. A snake that is blue may be more irritable during this time, which may be due to systemic changes or simply because it cannot see as well and therefore feels more easily threatened. After shedding, your specimen will again be as brightly hued and patterned as it was to begin with.

Although in the wild snakes seldom have problems shedding, some captives may. The problem may be due to the stress experienced by a new import, dehydration, starvation, or when the relative humidity in the terrarium or cage is too low.

How Shedding Is Accomplished

Generally speaking, the snake simply rubs its nose against a rock or limb in its cage to loosen the skin, then catches the edge of the skin against the rock or limb and crawls out of the old skin. It is important that no patches of old skin remain attached to the snake. If the snake seems to have difficulty in the shedding process, place it in a damp cloth bag overnight (make sure temperatures are regulated). This usually loosens the old skin and allows your snake to shed. Occasionally, you

Once the skin has loosened, the shedding process take just a few minutes.

As a snake crawls out of its old skin, the shed is inverted. Be very certain that the eyecaps are shed each time.

may have to manually help your snake rid itself of a particularly resistant shed.

Our tip: Remember that the clear eye covering, or eyecap, must be shed along with the skin. Examine the shed skin to make sure that the eyecaps have been shed. Sometimes the old skin may adhere to the tailtip or the eyes. If not manually (and very carefully) removed by the keeper, the dried skin can restrict circulation, resulting in the loss of the tailtip or, if on the eyes, impaired vision and eventual blindness. If patches of skin adhere, a gentle misting with tepid water may help your snake rid itself of the pieces. Use tweezers and caution to remove old eyecaps, if you cannot tell if the old eyecaps are in place don't hesitate to ask for help from someone more experienced.

Avoid shedding problems by elevating relative humidity, occasionally misting a snake that is preparing to shed, and keeping your rat snake in good health.

Quarantine

To avoid introducing diseases and parasites, quarantine new specimens. A month is best but even a week would be better than no quarantine at all. During quarantine, observe your new snake frequently. Check for mites (tiny, eight-legged parasites the size of a period) and ticks (larger ectoparasites, about a quarter-inch across). Watch for the usual danger signs—labored breathing, sneezing, or continual loose stools. Have a fecal specimen examined by a qualified reptile veterinarian before you place the new specimen with those already being maintained. If the specimen is wild-caught it might be hosting ticks that should be individually removed, or have an infestation of mites that must be immediately eradicated. The quarantine area should be completely removed from the area in which other reptiles are kept, preferably in another room. Wash your hands between handling either your quarantined or long-term specimens.

Keeping It Clean

Clean the quarantine terrarium prior to the introduction of the new snake(s) and regularly throughout the quarantine period. Use a weak Clorox solution or diluted alcohol spray for cleaning, and dry the tank before putting the specimen(s) back in. Gear the terrarium to the needs of the specimen in terms of temperature, feeding, humidity, size, lighting, and other factors such as the amount of space available.

The End of Quarantine

Once you (and your veterinarian) are completely satisfied that your new specimen(s) are healthy and habituated, they can be brought near other specimens.

Why bother? This quarantine period is important. It is during this period of isolation that you will be able to notice most health problems, whether established or incipient. Feeding schedules can be established, and your specimen can become at least semi-accustomed to the presence of people near its quarters. Quarantine can do a great deal toward preventing later health problems.

Reptilian veterinary medicine is a specialized field—not all veterinarians want to work on reptiles. We urge you to find a qualified veterinarian before you are in critical need of his or her services.

Health Problems and Treatment

Stress

Stress can cause problems in reptiles as well as in higher animals. Wild-collected snakes are more prone to stress-related problems than those that are captive-bred. The stress of collecting, shipping, and caging the snakes adds up, and you'll need to work to eliminate that stress. Provide a secure artificial habitat—a hidebox,

Use a non-phenol disinfectant to clean your cages.

perches, an adequate substrate, water, and food—and keep the rat snake's cage in a low-traffic area. You may need to temporarily tape newspaper over the front of the cage so your snake will feel more secure. High-strung species, like red-tailed green, the various stripe-tailed, and mandarin rat snakes, invariably show more stress-related problems than the calmer corn and black rat snake-complex animals. Doing all you can to reduce stress in captivity will help your rat snakes live long and healthy lives.

Burns, Bites, and Abscesses

Prevention of these problems requires some forethought on the part of the keeper.

Burns: Keep incandescent light bulbs and fixtures in a part of the cage your snake cannot reach, or cover the fixtures with a snake-proof wire cage.

Cover the front of the cage for nervous new acquisitions.

Make sure the surface of your hot rocks or blocks does not go above 95°F (35°C). If your snake sustains burns, cool the burned area and apply a clean, dry dressing until you take the snake to your veterinarian.

Bites: Rat snakes can be bitten by feed animals. Rats that are being constricted may bite, or a rodent left unattended in a snake's cage might chew on its predator, resulting in a snake being severely injured or permanently disfigured. These incidents are not uncommon, and are directly attributable to the snake owner's carelessness.

Avoid this by prekilling your rodents! Hold the prey by its tail and swing it so the head hits sharply against an edge of a counter or terrarium. Do not hope that your snake will make the kill cleanly and quickly—Someday it won't.

Rat snakes may bite each other during breeding. Males in a confined space competing for a female may bite each other as part of the courtship/dis-

play process, or the male may bite the female on the back of the neck during mating. If aggression continues, you may need to separate the snakes, but expect to get bitten yourself in the process. Remember not to jerk your hand too quickly when you're bitten—yanking back your hand may forcibly remove the teeth from the rat snake's jaw, resulting in infection. Common fabric garden gloves will help protect your hands, but again, move slowly.

Abscesses: An improperly sterilized and healed burn or bite on a rat snake can result in the formation of an abscess. Some will eventually heal and slough off or be rubbed off, and a very few may require surgical removal. Consult your reptile veterinarian.

Respiratory Problems

Snakes have only one working lung, and so it is mandatory that respiratory problems be identified and corrected. The cause may be bacterial, viral, or even due to a parasite. Be aware that a medication that works effectively on one species of snake might not work well on another, and some drugs that are ideally suited for curing a given respiratory problem may damage the snake's kidneys if the animal is dehydrated in the least. Some bacteria are resistant to traditional antibiotics, such as ampicillin, amoxicillin, tetracycline, or penicillin.

What to do: It is crucial that you have a veterinarian determine the sensitivity of the bacteria present. If a respiratory ailment worsens, it can be fatal. You can help by elevating the cage temperature and reducing the relative humidity. Since some respiratories are communicable, quarantine the sick snake in a separate cage, preferably in a separate room.

Infectious Stomatitis (Mouth Rot)

An insidious and common disease, uncorrected mouth rot can result in permanent disfigurement, if not death. Stress, mouth injuries, and unsanitary caging conditions cause this disease. Characterized by areas of white, cheesy-looking exudate along the snake's gums, this material may be massive enough to force the lips apart. Your snake is not comfortable. Once detected, the mouth should be cleaned of the exudate. Use cotton swabs, then wash the affected areas with hydrogen peroxide. Sulfa drugs (sulfamethazine seems to be the drug of choice) are effective against the bacteria that cause the disease. A veterinarian may suggest that you use an antibiotic as well. Complete eradication of mouth rot can take up to two weeks of daily treatment.

Blister Disease

To diagnose: If your rat snake's skin has tiny white raised spots or nodules, you are both in trouble. Although this skin problem is usually associated with dirty water and unclean quarters (more rarely with parasites), blister disease sometimes crops up simply when the humidity in a cage is overly high or when the substrate is kept wet. This can be a fatal disease if not caught and treated promptly.

Treatment: If the problem is caused by mites, clean the cage and follow the instructions for combatting mites on page 20.

For blister disease caused by too-damp quarters, start by cleaning and sterilizing the cage. Change the substrate, put in a smaller water bowl, and remove any plants. Make sure you maintain the cage in these new clean standards.

If the blister disease is not well advanced, and if the causative agents are eliminated, your snake will now enter a rapid shed cycle and rid itself of the problems within two or three sheds.

If the disease is advanced, with underlying tissue damage, it will be necessary to rupture each blister and clean the area daily (for seven to fourteen days) with dilute Betadine and/or hydrogen peroxide. Again, your snake will enter a rapid shed cycle and after two sheds its skin should appear normal.

Ectoparasites

Ticks: Snakes from the wild, as well as captive specimens, can bear mites and ticks. Ticks are easier to deal with because they are bigger and present in only small concentrations, and so are readily seen and removed. To remove a tick, very carefully coat it first with Vaseline or dab it with alcohol. (Use a cotton swab if you don't want to use your fingers.) After a few minutes, the tick's grip will loosen, and you can use tweezers to gently pull the tick out. Check that the sucking mouthparts are removed intact, and crush the arachnid before disposing of it.

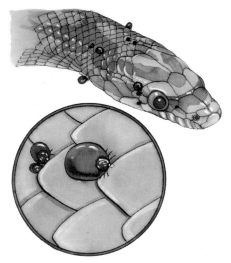

Ticks fasten their mouthparts between scales.

Mites: These are more difficult to combat since they're smaller and often present in immense numbers. A pervasive airborne insecticide such as that contained in a "no-pest strip" is an excellent combatant that alleviates the necessity of handling the snake. Remove the water dish and hang a square (about one inch [2.5 cm] on each side for a ten-gallon [38L] tank, 1 inch × 2 inch [2.5 × 5 cm] for a 20 (76L), etc.) in a perforated container either in the terrarium or placed on top of the screen lid. Your snake must not be allowed to come in contact with the strip. Leave the strip in place for three to four days, remove it (you can store it in a glass jar with a tightly fitting lid), and replace the water dish. Since the strip does not kill mite eggs, it will be necessary to treat the snake and its enclosure a second time, nine days later, when the mite eggs have hatched. An alternate treatment is injectable Ivermectin, which can be administered by your veterinarian.

Place a piece of no-pest strip atop the cage to destroy mites.

Endoparasites

Diagnosis and treatment: Many reptiles, even those that are captive-bred and hatched, can harbor internal parasites. When present in sufficient numbers, parasites will cause abnormal stools (loose, watery, mucousy, or bloody). Fecal smears and floats, and smears taken from the mucosa, should be periodically performed by a qualified veterinarian to determine whether endoparasites are present. If so, they must be eradicated. Because of the difficulties in identifying endoparasites and the need to administer purge dosages by the weight of the snake, ridding your snake of internal parasites is best left to a qualified reptile veterinarian. The presence of the following information is in no way intended to promote home diagnoses and medications. The tables should be considered only as they are intended, as a guideline. Below are a few of the recommended medications and dosages.

Amoebas and Trichomonads

40–50 mg/kg of **Metronidazole** orally, once a day. The treatment is repeated in two weeks.

Dimetridazole can also be used but the dosage is very different: 40–50 mg/kg of Dimetrizadole is administered daily for five days. The treatment is then repeated in two weeks.

Coccidia

Many treatments are available. The dosages of **sulfadiazine, sulfamerazine**, and **sulfamethazine** are identical: administer 75 mg/kg the first day, then follow up for the next five days with 45 mg/kg. All treatments orally and once daily.

Sulfadimethoxine is also effective. The initial dosage is 90 mg/kg orally to be followed on the next five days with 45 mg/kg orally. All dosages are administered once daily.

Medical abbreviations

mg —milligram
(1 mg = 0.001 gram)
kg —kilogram
(1000 grams; 2.2 pounds)
mcg —microgram
(1 mcg = 0.000001 gram)
IM —intramuscularly
IP —intraperitoneally
PO —orally

Trimethoprim-sulfa may also be used: 30 mg/kg should be administered once daily for seven days.

Cestodes (=Tapeworms)

Several effective treatments are available.

Bunamidine may be administered orally at a dosage of 50 mg/kg; a second treatment is given in 14 days.

Niclosamide, orally, at a dosage of 150 mg/kg, is also effective; a second treatment is given in two weeks.

Praziquantel may be administered either orally or intramuscularly. The dosage is 5–8 mg/kg and is to be repeated in 14 days.

Trematodes (Flukes)

Praziquantel, at 8 mg/kg, may be administered either orally or intramuscularly; the treatment is repeated in two weeks.

Nematodes (Roundworms)

Several effective treatments are available.

Levamisole, an injectable intraperitoneal treatment, should be administered at a dosage of 10 mg/kg; the treatment is repeated in two weeks.

Ivermectin, injected intramuscularly in a dosage of 200 mcg/kg is effective. The treatment is to be repeated in two weeks. Ivermectin can be toxic to certain taxa.

Thiabendazole and **Fenbendazole** have similar dosages. Both are administered orally at 50–100 mg/kg and repeated in 14 days.

Mebendazole is administered orally at a dosage of 20–25 mg/kg and repeated in 14 days.

Naturally occurring color variations may be seen among most of the rat snakes. This is an aberrant yellow rat snake from Lee County, Florida.

Caging Your Rat Snake

These general descriptions pertain to housing for most of the "easier" rat snake species and subspecies. Among these are various subspecies of corn, black, and Baird's rat snakes (*E. guttata* ssp., *E. obsoleta* ssp., *E. bairdi*, respectively), many of the beauty or striped-tailed rat snakes, *E. taeniura* subspecies, and other species of similar size. For some of the more difficult species, see the various species accounts in this book (beginning on page 43).

Today, buying caging for snakes is as easy as going to your local pet store, where cages made specifically for snakes are available, as well as aquarium tanks that may be converted into perfectly acceptable reptile terraria. Choosing the basic tank is an

easy procedure—the difficult part will be deciding how elaborate you want the cage to be, which is directly related to how much time you want to spend on cage maintenance.

Simple "American-Style" Caging

Over the years, American herpeto-culturists have become known for caging snakes in the simplest, most utilitarian manner possible. American hobbyists usually opt for the bare minimum when setting up a cage. Many hobbyists begin with an empty aquarium tank or plastic shoebox and add little more than an absorbent bottom of folded newspaper, paper towels, or aspen shavings, an untippable water bowl, and a hidebox. The hardier rat snakes species seem to thrive, and some (such as corn snakes) will even breed, in such Spartan quarters.

• Plastic shoe, sweater, and blanket boxes are available in many hardware and department stores. Be sure the lids fit securely, or can be secured with tape or velcro strips. Aquaria, of course, are available in virtually any pet department and screen lids are a standard stock item.

If plastic caging is used, sufficient air (ventilation) holes must be drilled (or melted) through the sides to provide adequate air transfer and to prevent excessive humidity from building up within. We prefer ventilation on at least two sides, often on all four sides. If an arid climate rat snake is being kept, we ventilate the top as well.

• Shelving systems that hold a dozen or more plastic boxes are now available, many with heat tapes built in. These are

A simple aquarium tank makes a good terrarium.

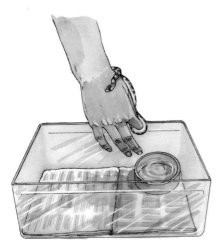

Smaller snakes may be kept in plastic shoe or sweater boxes.

Use a soldering gun to melt ventilation holes in a plastic shoe or sweater box.

advertised in most reptile magazines and at many of the reptile meets.

• Glass aquaria can be oriented in either a normal horizontal or a vertical position, as desired. If you opt for a vertical orientation, the clip-on screen top can serve as a side. Glue feet on the side of the tank serving as the bottom, so the top is easy to take off and put on. If you prefer, you can construct a vertical system from two tanks of the same size. After accidentally breaking the bottom of what had been a standard 15-gallon (56.7L) tank, and then placing that tank on top of another, we found we could easily "construct" vertically oriented terraria that are ideal for arboreal rat snakes.

• Custom glass terraria can either be purchased or, if you are just the slightest bit handy, can be built by you. Merely take your measurements, cut the pieces of glass (or have them cut), and using a latex aquarium sealant, build your custom tank. The glass can be held in place with strips of tape while the sealant is curing (about 24 hours). The most important thing when using the latex is to make absolutely

certain that the edges of the glass that are to be sealed are completely free of any oils or any other debris that could prevent the aquarium sealant from forming a tight seal. Remarkably large terraria can be held together very securely with aquarium sealant, especially if the tanks will not be intended to hold water.

Shelving units are commercially available for multiple caging.

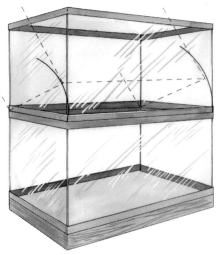

Remove the bottom of one tank and stack and seal the two for a tall terrarium.

"European-Style" Caging

In direct contrast to the starkness preferred by most American hobbyists, their European counterparts have become well known for the intricacy of detail that goes into the construction of their terrarium interiors. The Europeans, it seems, prefer to

A European terrarium can be a work of art.

reconstruct a little corner of nature, a working, miniaturized ecosystem, in their terraria. This concept has stood the Europeans in good stead, for several rat snake species, considered difficult-to-impossible by most American hobbyists, are rather routinely bred (if only in small numbers) by continental herpetoculturists. The European concept is to fit the terrarium setting to the species in question.

Pros: In reality, both the American and European concepts have their places. It is far easier to care for large numbers of specimens in the rather sterile, generic cages in which they are kept by the Americans than in the intricate terraria of the European hobbyists.

Cons: To successfully create a terrarium of the European style takes knowledge, time, and dedication—you do not only need an understanding of your rat snakes, but an understanding of the dynamics of their habitat as well. You then must move a cross-section of that habitat indoors, establish it, and keep it viable. It is not an easy task.

Additionally, although it is a more natural setting that is more conducive to normal (whatever that means) behavior by the snakes, it may actually be more difficult to maintain ideal conditions in a European-style setup than in one of the less intricate American ones. If the naturalistic terrarium is too damp, too dry, or has incorrect lighting, not only will the vegetation suffer, but the serpentine inhabitants can also.

Inside the Cage

Cage Furniture

Many rat snakes are climbers—especially within the confines of captivity. However, climbing requires the firm stability provided by sizable limbs, not the uncertainty of pliant twigs. Limbs need to be at least one and a half times the diameter of the snake's body. Limbs, cut to the exact inside length of the terrarium, can be secured at any level with thick U-shaped beads of aquarium sealant that have been placed on the aquarium glass. Merely slide the limb downward into the open top of the U until the limb rests securely in place.

Other cage furniture, whether naturalistic or "plastic functional," can be used.

Hiding

Rat snakes enjoy (and some need) hiding areas for seclusion and security. This is especially true if the cage is located in a heavily trafficked area and the inhabitant is one of the nervous species.
• Preformed plastic caves are readily available at many pet and reptile dealers. These are washable and sterilizable, and will last for years.
• Parakeet and cockatiel nesting boxes are readily accepted by most species of rat snakes.
• A disposable cardboard box (like a shoebox) with an access hole cut in one end will also provide shelter.
• We provide natural-looking hollow limbs that we pick up as we find them

Rat snakes like small, darkened hide-areas. Two 20″ long stripe-tailed rat snakes rest comfortably in a film-box.

in woods and fields. These can be used as floor furnishings or can be Silastic-secured at suitable levels in the terraria.
• Corkbark is a reasonable alternative to the hollow limbs and is much lighter, more impervious to body wastes, and easily cleaned and sterilized for lengthy use. It is available at many pet stores, reptile dealers, and plant nurseries.

Secure the tree limbs with aquarium sealant.

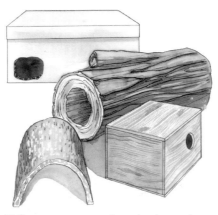

Hiding areas can purchased or be made from corkbark, cardboard boxes, hollow limbs, or bird nesting boxes.

Lighting, Heating, and a Comment on Weather Patterns

Staying Warm

Snakes, being ectothermic (the old term was *cold-blooded*) creatures, regulate their body temperatures by utilizing outside sources of heating and cooling. At most times, they warm themselves by choosing a secluded place and basking in the sun. When they are preparing to shed and vision is impaired, they are more secretive and seek warmed areas beneath litter (discarded sheets of plywood and rusted roofing tin are two favored examples) or under natural cover such as flat rocks. In areas with rocky ledges or hollowed fallen trees, the snakes may merely rest in the entryway of their denning area and extend a coil or two of body out into the sun.

While tropical and semitropical rat snakes may remain active the year around, northern snakes hibernate (brumate). Snakes in areas that are subject to only periodic cold spells

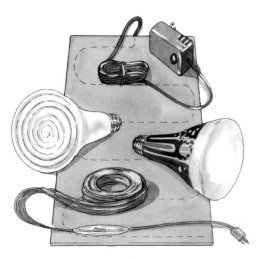

Heat sources include incadescent bulbs, commercial heat "coils," or a heating pad or heating tapes under one end of the cage.

may become dormant only during those cold spells. Even though semi-active, these snakes may not feed for most of the cooler time of the year.

Staying Cool

Although different snake species have adapted to different environments, it is as important for snakes to remain comfortably cool as warm. During hot weather, or where temperatures are naturally very hot (southwestern deserts), rat snakes are either nocturnal or may aestivate (undergo a period of warm weather dormancy) through the weeks of excessive heat.

Weather and Behavior

Naturally changing weather patterns—dry seasons, rainy seasons, low pressure frontal systems, the high pressure associated with fine weather, and even the lunar cycle, are known to affect snake behavior. Rat snakes are often most active during the dark of the moon, during unsettled weather, and at the changing of the tropical seasons (from wet to dry or, more common, vice versa). Reproductive behavior is often stimulated by the lowering barometric pressures that occur at the advent of a storm, and the increase in humidity.

Natural light cycles are nearly as important to the snakes as temperature. Under normal conditions, snake activity is greatest during the longest days of the year (which just happen to coincide with the most optimum temperatures as well). Those snakes that hibernate do so during the shortest days of the year.

Thermoregulation is important even for captive snakes. They, of course, are then dependent on us, their keepers, to provide them with caging that permits them to select their body temperature. Warming the cage can be done with heating pads, heating tapes, and hot rocks, although the latter are not particularly recommended. Ceramic heating units that screw into a light socket, and lightbulbs (especially those with directed beams such as flood and spot lights) are other possible sources of heat, and the bulbs provide light as well as heat. Fluorescent bulbs will provide light but little heat, which can be advantageous when you live in a warmer area where not much additional heat is needed.

Provide thermal gradients except during hibernation when the terrarium temperature should be uniformly cool (see the species account for *Senticolis triaspis intermedia*, page 63, for what may be the sole exception to this statement). Keep one end of the tank cool (preferably 65–75°F [18–24°C]) and provide heat at the other end. The warm end of the tank can be between 75–82°F [24–28°C] (for rat snakes from high altitude or northern climes), to as high as 88–95°F (31–35°C) for warmth-loving species. See the species accounts, beginning on page 43, for specific temperature suggestions. In small tanks, we put the hide-box on the cool end of the tank. If the tank is sufficiently large, we put a hide-box on both ends.

Caution: Make certain that whatever heating unit you choose is thermostatically controlled. Please note that, while the current type of heat rocks is more reliable than its predecessors, serious thermal burns have occurred during use. If it is your choice to use a heat rock, monitor it carefully.

Full-Spectrum/Ultraviolet Light

We are often asked whether we feel ultraviolet illumination is necessary for rat snakes. Our answer must be that while it may not be absolutely mandatory, it sure can't hurt. We provide full-spectrum lighting above each cage. While the amount of UV supplied may be negligible, the color-temperature of full-spectrum bulbs—a means

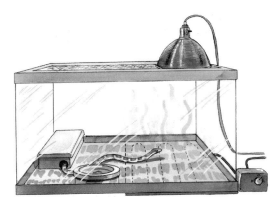

Each cage should have a warm and a cool area.

by which the amount of natural sunlight-like light is measured—may be beneficial to captive snakes.

Rather than heat/cool/light individual cages, some very successful hobbyists treat large collections of species with similar needs, even if individually caged, as a single unit. The temperature of the entire room is thermostatically controlled. Lighting is controlled to yield a natural/normal photoperiod (usually 16 hours of daylight in the summer and 10 hours of daylight in the winter—check the sunrise/sunset times in your daily paper for seasonal shifts). This means that the room/cage is illuminated during the daylight hours and darkened at night. While this is effective for most of the easily kept, nondemanding rat snakes, it seems less satisfactory for many of the more specialized European and Asiatic species. Montane and lowland species differ in their high and low temperature requirements.

Water, Soaking Bowls, and Cage Humidity

Although the several arid climate (desert and savanna) forms of rat snakes may drink and soak less often than the more humidity-tolerant "typical" species, water is important to all.

Using Differing Sizes of Water Bowls to Change Cage Humidity

If you live in an area with an average humidity of:

and you are keeping	40%<	41–60%	61–80%	80%>
B. subocularis	M 7	M 7	S 2	S 2
E. guttata	L 7	L 7	L 7	L 7
E. obsoleta	L 7	L 7	L 7	L 7
E. situla	M 7	M 7	S 2	S 2
E. taeniura	L 7	L 7	L 7	L 7
S. triaspis	M 7	M 7	S 2	S 2

Water bowl size: S = small, M = medium, L = large
Weekly water bowl access: 1 through 7 (# of days/week water is available)

Cage humidity can be an important consideration in successful maintenance. Species from humid areas will have shedding problems if the humidity is too low; species from desert areas can develop serious (even fatal) health problems if humidity is too high. In the latter case, hobbyists have found that species such as Trans-Pecos and Baja California rat snakes—two of the most aridland dwelling species—may languish if kept in the perpetual high humidity of our southeastern coastal plain states.

Besides serving as a drinking receptacle, the water bowl can play an integral part in raising or lowering the humidity in a cage. Cage humidity will be higher in a cage lacking adequate ventilation than in one with more adequate air circulation. See the box at the top of this page.

If you wish to increase, then retain, a high humidity in your cage, place the water bowl in the hottest spot (over a heating pad if one is being used). If you wish to decrease, or keep humidity as low as possible, situate the water bowl in the coolest spot in the cage.

Please note: If your snake is *opaque* or *blue*, the condition assumed prior to skin-shedding, you may wish to have a water dish large enough for your snake to soak in the cage at all times. Also, snakes often prowl actively when they are thirsty. It is best to allow your snake an opportunity to drink if it seems excessively active.

Red-tailed green rat snake, Gonyosoma oxycephalum.

Feeding and Food for Your Rat Snake

The Mechanics of Feeding

Rat snakes find their prey primarily by feel, sight, and scent. They can, apparently, see moving objects rather well (there is some question about whether snakes perceive stationary objects), and quickly orient on them visually. In addition to sight, vibrations are noted and a rat snake's sense of smell is quite acute. Air- and ground-borne cues are carried by the tongue of the rat snake to the sensory Jacobson's organs (see Glossary, page 99) nestled in the palate where the odors are sorted out. Besides determining the presence and kind of prey (either alive or dead) in the vicinity, odors from other snakes (pheromones) play a tremendous part in the breeding behavior of rat snakes.

After grasping its prey in its jaws, a rat snake overpowers its prey in one of two ways: by constriction (an effective method), or by throwing a loop of body over it and holding the prey animal as immobile as possible.

Constriction

Constriction does not result in broken bones or other such structural damage to the prey. Rather, with each exhalation of the prey animal, the constricting coils of the snake are tightened. Soon, inhalation is impossible and the prey suffocates. Snake critics feel that this is a cruel death, but we can only state that Mother Nature is efficient, not kind, and it seems probable that most prey animals go into shock nearly immediately. However, since we care about humane treatment of both predators and prey, we feed prekilled animals to all snakes that will accept them. Rat snakes are well capable of constricting two or more prey items at the same time; two separate constricting coils can be employed simultaneously. At times, prey may be pushed by a coil against the sides of a burrow or tree hollow. This is nearly as efficient a method of overpowering prey as actual constriction.

Positioning and Swallowing

Once the snake determines that the prey is ready to be eaten, positioning and swallowing begins. The snake may

Two of the four upper tooth rows are visible on this feeding yellow rat snake.

29

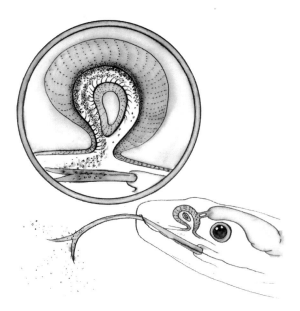

Snakes use their tongues to transport scent to the Jacobson's organ in the mouth.

entirely release its hold on the prey, or, with flickering tongue carrying chemical cues to the Jacobson's organs, retain its hold but search out the head or, more rarely, the feet, to begin the swallowing process.

Nearly everything about a snake, beginning with the jaw structure, is "elastic." All tooth-bearing bones, both upper and lower, are capable of independent movement. Designed to retain a hold, the conical teeth are all recurved. To swallow its prey, the snake (usually) extends the upper and lower jaw bones on one side forward, in order to gain a purchase on the prey. The same sequence now occurs with the opposite side. Once inside the throat, contractions of the neck push the prey into the stomach of the snake. In essence, the snake "walks" its way around the prey animal. According to temperature and the metabolism of the snake, digestion may be slow or rather rapid. During this time, the snake is quieter than usual, often moving no further than is necessary to effectively thermoregulate.

Diet

Contrary to conventional wisdom, snakes do not feed entirely on live food, nor do some even prefer it. We have seen rat snakes in the wild find and eat long-dead rodents. We feed our captive rat snakes thawed, once-frozen mice and rats.

Though called rat snakes, the diets of none of these creatures is strictly limited to rats. For that matter, few of the species even limit their diets to the acceptance of endothermic (warm-blooded) prey. The diets of many of the rat snakes change with the age of the snakes. In the wild, the juveniles of many seek lizards and frogs for their first few meals. With increasing size, there is more of a tendency for most rat snakes to become opportunistic feeders and their diets are expanded to include nestling birds, eggs, and suitably sized rodents.

Where a particular fondness for a specific food item is known, it is mentioned in the individual species account (see, for example, the comments made regarding the fondness of *E. rufodorsata* for fish and frogs, page 89).

We suggest that you offer prey that is sized to the snake: pinkies or lizards to hatchlings or small snakes, those less than 14 inches long (35.5 cm); furred "jumpers" to snakes between 14 and 18 inches long; small mice for young adult rat snakes 18 to 22 inches (45.7 cm) long; and adult mice or young rats to snakes larger than 22 inches (55.8 cm).

How Frequently to Feed

This depends on the snake and the time of year. During the summer months, rat snakes generally eat every week or every second week. During the winter months, those that do not actually hibernate will nonetheless greatly decrease their food intake, to once every three weeks, or once a month, or even less frequently. Remember that snakes evolved along with their prey, and their appetites are closely attuned to the natural occurrences of their prey. Food is scarcer during the winter months.

What to Feed

Mice, rats and other rodents, anoles, and, sometimes, tree frogs are rather generally available at pet shops and specialty dealers across the United States, Europe, and in many areas of Asia. Often, "feed" rodents and lizards are considerably cheaper than "pet" rodents or lizards. Frozen rodents may be cheaper yet. Compare prices.

Because of the ease with which domestic mice and rats may be had, there is a tendency for hobbyists to try to induce even hatchling snakes to accept rodent fare. While this is acceptable, it is probably not natural, and although long lives are attained by our captive snakes, many herpetoculturists (us included) wonder how much better we would do (especially with "difficult" rat snake species) if we strived more toward a natural diet.

Prekilled Food

Prekilled food items are suggested. A live rodent or bird can bite or peck a captive snake, causing additional stress to the snake or even irreversible damage. We generally buy bulk lots of frozen mice from a reptile dealer and thaw the number needed in warm water (after which we blot them dry with paper towels), or at room temperature, or beneath a snake's basking lamp at feeding time. Because of hot spots, partial cooking, and deterioration of the body wall, don't use a microwave for thawing.

Buying prekilled, frozen mice "by the bag" is an easy way to provide food for your rat snakes.

Using Wild Prey

We are often asked about the wisdom of feeding wild rodents (especially mice) to rat snakes. We feel that there are three points that you should consider when making a decision:
• you must be absolutely certain that the wild rodent has ingested no rat or mouse poisons;
• be aware that wild rodents or their fleas can be carriers of certain serious diseases that are transmissible to humans;
• once they have eaten wild rodents, some rat snakes like them so much that they may be reluctant to accept domestic types again.

On the positive side, some rat snakes that are reluctant to feed on domestic rodents will eagerly accept wild species. We breed white-footed mice for just such contingencies.

Breeding Your Own Food Rodents

Although readily available at pet and specialty shops, some people breed their own food rodents. Most are easily bred, but breed best if maintained at comfortable room temperatures. If too cold or too hot, breeding

A small mouse colony of one male and two females will generally provide enough pinkies and young mice to feed two small rat snakes or one young rat snake.

Wild mice, such as these white-footed mice, are eagerly eaten by some reluctant feeders.

ceases or, if it continues, litters are smaller and cannibalism of the new-borns is likely. Of all rodents, mice are the most easily bred and the most universally accepted by snakes. A single male to three or four female mice may be housed in a ten-gallon tank or a rodent breeding cage. This type of colony will produce a rather steady supply of babies that can be fed to your smaller snakes, or allowed to size up for the larger specimens. The colony will also produce a distinct odor, so clean the cages at least twice weekly. Since even clean cages have an odor, locate the cages away from your home if possible. A temperature-controlled garage is often ideal for a colony or two. Use aspen or pine shavings for the bedding. (Do *not* use cedar bedding for your mice as the phenols contained in cedar can be harmful to your rat snakes.)

Feeding Your Rodents

Feed your mice either a "lab-chow" diet that is specifically formulated for them or a healthy mixture of seeds and vegetables. Fresh water must be present at all times. Snakes will derive the most benefit from healthy prey.

Gerbils and hamsters can also be raised in small cages. Rats will do better if they are in somewhat larger facilities.

Certain wild mice can also be bred in captivity. Among the most frequently raised are deer and white-footed mice. (However, keep in mind our caution about rodent-borne diseases mentioned earlier on page 31.)

Above: It is hard to resist some of the names given captive bred intergrade rat snakes. This "bubblegum" rat snake was bred and photographed by Bill Love of Glades Herp.
Top left: Everglades rat snake, Elaphe obsoleta rossalleni.
Top right: Eastern fox snake, Elaphe gloydi.
Middle left: Bubblegum rat snake, E. o. rossalleni x E. o. obsoleta.
Bottom left: Some specimens of Baird's rat snakes from Texas can be an attractive pearl gray in coloration.

HOW-TO:
Inducing a Reluctant Feeder

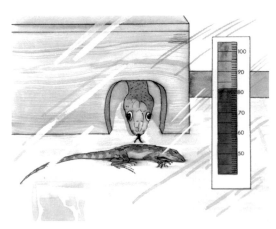

A shy snake may accept prekilled prey items left at the door of its hidebox.

Try Varying the Prey

Experiment with offering prey items of different species and colors. Some snakes will readily accept a newly born rat pup, but will steadfastly refuse a mouse of similar bulk. If they will accept neither rat nor mouse, try a hamster or a gerbil.

For hatchling or juvenile rat snakes, first try pinky mice, then pinky mice scented with tree frog or lizard odors, then tree frogs or lizards. Subadult and adult rat snakes may accept the most conveniently available rodents (mice, rats, gerbils, hamsters). Then try baby chicks and/or button quail.

Try feeding a reluctant feeder during its major activity period. Some rat snakes are nocturnally active; some are diurnal. Check the species accounts for natural history notes. A secure snake will feed more readily than one that is stressed. Provide a hidebox of some sort (see page 25) and place a prekilled food item in the doorway of the box.

Make sure that your snake is kept at its optimum temperature. A rat snake that is stressed by being overly warm, or that is lethargic from temperatures that are too cool, cannot be expected to eat, nor will it usually do so. Regurgitation is also caused by unsuitable maintenance temperatures.

If your snake eats willingly, but prefers lizards over mice, scent the mouse with lizard's blood or even feces. We will often break the readily autotomized tail (which quickly regrows) off of an anole, smear the droplet of serum that accompanies the break on the snout of a suitably sized mouse, and release the lizard. Rat snakes will frequently accept the scented mouse.

Keep the Meals Small

Small prey animals (whether alive or dead) are often more readily accepted by a rat snake than large ones. Two small prey items are more easily digested by the snake than one large food animal.

Small meals are also swallowed by snakes more easily and quickly. While this may make no difference to a well-adjusted specimen that feeds readily, if a nervous specimen or a poor feeder becomes

It may be necessary to try a variety of food animals to induce a reluctant feeder to eat.

Place the food item far back in the snake's mouth, close the mouth, and wait to see if the snake will voluntarily swallow the item.

stressed while eating, the snake is apt to lose the urge to feed or to disgorge a partially swallowed prey item.

Force Feeding As a Last Resort

Despite all of your efforts, there is the occasional rat snake that will not voluntarily accept an offered food item. In these cases, there is little recourse but to force feed the specimen. Remember, the digestive system of a snake that has not fed in some time is probably compromised. Do *not* overfeed such a specimen. In fact, initially *underfeed* it. A compromised, basically nonfunctioning digestive system will be better able to digest a proportionately small meal than a large one. In force feeding, you may use a "pinky pump"—a metal syringe with a large diameter needle. Put pieces of pinkies inside the barrel of the pump. Lubricate the tip before inserting it down the throat (into the esophagus) of the snake. The unenhanced length of the tip of the pinky pump will allow sufficient insertion to feed a baby snake. If the pump is being used to feed a larger specimen, it may be necessary to affix a longer piece of smooth plastic tube to allow insertion for an additional distance. Use care—do not injure the gums, teeth, mouth-lining, or glottis.

Another alternative is to actually place a small prekilled food animal far back into the snake's mouth and massage the food down the snake's throat. First, lubricate the mouse with water (some hobbyists prefer egg white). Next, insert the head of the rodent gently into the mouth of the snake. If done slowly and gently, the head of the mouse can be used to open the mouth of the snake. If at any time while you are doing this the snake begins to voluntarily swallow, slowly release your grip and allow the snake to eat voluntarily. Often the snake will volunteer nothing and it will be necessary to slowly work the prey animal into and beyond the throat of the snake. Once pushed gently past the angle of the mouth, you will be able to work the rodent downward by gently massaging anterior to its position in the snake. If the snake shows little resistance, gently release it and see if it will work the prey into its stomach. If it begins to try to regurgitate, gently grasp the snake and massage the prey to a position a little closer to the snake's stomach.

Caution: In either case, force feeding is traumatic for the snake and requires the utmost care on your part when it is being accomplished. Move *slowly!* This is important, for a startled snake is quite apt to fight the force feeding or to regurgitate the meal once it *is* force fed.

Do remember that the snake will have to be mostly immobilized during force feeding. Even force feeding may not always save a seriously debilitated snake, but it *is* worth making the effort.

Breeding Your Rat Snakes

At the outset, we would like to state that the guidelines given here or in the species accounts for breeding or cycling your rat snakes are just that— guidelines. These methods have worked for us in our facility in south- western Florida. There we could suc- cessfully incubate many eggs at "room temperature" (always between 79 and 89°F [26–32°C], but most often between 82 and 86°F [28–30°C]), and we had to strive to reduce the relative humidity in the cages of arid climate species and to provide suitably cool incubating temperatures for those species that did require full hibernation (or brumation—the terms are inter- changeable) for reproductive cycling. Hobbyists and commercial breeders in the Pacific Northwest find it necessary to strive to attain additional warmth for the majority of the year, and those in California or other areas of the Southwest need to accomplish differ- ent parameters for their operations. Thus, we emphasize the word *guide- lines*. An old adage best states the sit- uation: "If it ain't broke, don't fix it." In other words, if you or a friend are suc- cessfully breeding rat snakes of a given species in a given area by using given methods, stick with *your* pro- gram. Herpetoculture is fraught with vagaries—what works well for one hobbyist may not be equally success- ful for another. But please share your methods with other hobbyists who have similar interests.

Getting Started

The basics for breeding rat snakes are not complex, and a few general guidelines will give you enough infor- mation to begin. More detailed infor- mation is in the species accounts, beginning on page 43.

Very briefly, you'll need both a male and a female rat snake, prefer- ably of the same type. In an ideal situation, when placed together in the early spring, the snakes will mate. The female will lay her eggs, which will hatch in 60 or so days. The babies will then have enough time before

To provide a resting period for your rat snake, reduce the lighting, cool the cage by switching off auxiliary heat and/or open- ing a window, or by moving the cage to a cooler area.

winter's cooler weather and shortened days to feed and put on some weight.

Resting or hibernation? Rat snakes from a more northerly area or a higher altitude generally need an annual cooling period to trigger the breeding response. Rat snakes from southern areas may need no annual cooling, or only a 30-day "rest" period. Find out where your snake originated and research the climatic conditions and microhabitats of that area to determine whether your snake needs cooling or brumation. Hatchlings should not be brumated or "rested" during the first year.

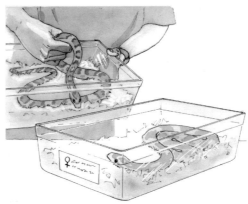

Covered plastic shoe or sweater boxes serve well as hibernating receptacles.

Providing a Resting Period for Your Rat Snake

1. For those species that do not require a complete hibernation, reduce ambient temperatures by switching from incandescent to fluorescent lights, turning off heating pads, opening room windows, or moving the cage to a cooler area. Daytime temperatures of 78–83°F (26–28°C) and nighttime temperatures of 66–70°F (19–21°C) are usually adequately cool.

2. Use a natural photoperiod. If there is sufficient lighting from outside, the photoperiod will be no problem. If not, use a timer keyed to the sunrise/sunset times listed in your newspaper or from your local library.

3. Keep water available at all times and feed smaller meals at greater intervals.

At the end of the 30 days, restore your usual caging temperatures and return to your usual feeding schedule. After a week or so, place the male and female snakes together. Breeding generally ensues.

Hibernating Your Rat Snake

1. Separate the sexes.
2. Stop feeding two weeks prior to

cooling. Do not feed during the cooling period.

3. Reduce relative humidity by removing items from the cage that retain moisture, such as plants and the water dish. Alternatively, prepare a plastic container, such as a shoebox, to serve as the hibernation quarters.

4. Clear a shelf in a cool, little-used closet in a basement or garage for the hibernation cages. Snakes need steady darkness and very cool temperatures for hibernation.

Hibernating snakes should be provided with cool temperatures and darkness.

HOW-TO:
Making Your Own Incubator

Materials Needed for One Incubator
- 1 wafer thermostat/heater (obtainable from feed stores; these are commonly used in incubators for chicks)
- 1 thermometer
- 1 heat tape (obtained from hardware or garden stores)
- 1 styrofoam cooler (one with thick sides—a fish shipping box is ideal)

Directions
1. Poke a hole through the lid of the styro cooler, and suspend the thermostat/heater from the inside. Add another hole for a thermometer so you can check the inside temperature without opening the top. If there's no flange on the thermometer to keep it from slipping through the hole in the lid, use a rubber band wound several times around the thermometer to form a flange.

2. Transverse the bottom of the cooler with the heat tape and wire the tape to the thermostat.

3. Put the lid on the cooler, and plug in the thermostat/heater. Wait half an hour, then check the temperature. Adjust the thermostat/heater until the temperature inside the incubator is about 80 to 86°F (27–30°C) (see the species accounts beginning on page 43 so you'll

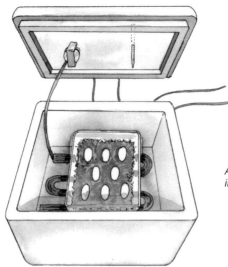

A homemade incubator is inexpensive to construct.

know what temperature to use). The L-pin "handle" on the top of the thermostat is the rheostat.

4. Once you have the temperature regulated, put the container of eggs inside the incubator and close the lid.

5. Check the temperature daily and add a little water to the incubating medium as needed. The preferred humidity is 100%, which can be accomplished by keeping the hatching medium of peat and soil damp to the touch but too dry to squeeze out any water by hand.

Fertile Eggs
How do you know if the eggs are fertile? By the end of the first week, those eggs that are *not* fertile will turn yellow, harden, and begin to collapse. Those that *are* fertile will remain white and turgid to the touch. Infertile eggs may mold, but this is seldom transferred to healthy eggs.

The Babies
At the end of the incubation period—which may be as little as two weeks for some species, but is usually 60–70 days—the baby snakes will cut a slit in their egg with the egg tooth on the tip of their snout.

The babies do not seem eager to leave the egg. They will cut a slit, look out, and decide to stay inside the egg for a while longer, perhaps as long as a day and a half. Those that leave the egg can be removed to another terrarium and offered food, a sunning spot, and water. They should shed within a few days.

Live rodents can injure your snake. Acclimate your snake to prekilled prey.

Although a single small incubator will be sufficiently large for most hobbyists, with expansion, and breeding success, you may need a larger unit.

5. Hibernation temperatures should be between 48 and 56°F (9.5–13°C).

6. Hibernating specimens should be roused for a drink every 15 days or so. Take the snake out of its box, place it on a shelf in front of you, and offer it water. After it drinks, place it back into its hibernation quarters. (Do not allow the snake to warm to room temperature.) If the snake does not drink, return it to its hibernation quarters and re-offer it water in a week.

7. At the end of the hibernation period, simply replace your snake in its regular caging with water dish, hiding box, limbs, and plants, etc., in place.

Courtship

Allow the snake a week or so to warm up, wake up completely, and readjust to its usual surroundings; then offer a meal of the accustomed food. Most, if not all, rat snakes will shed their skin soon after emerging from hibernation. Following the post-hibernation shed, the snakes cycle reproductively. If the sexes are still separated, now is the time to put them together. If courtship does not begin, mist the cage with a simple sprayer bottle. Point the bottle upwards so the mist falls like a gentle spring rain.

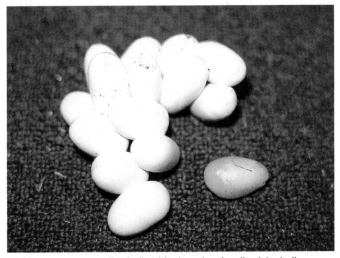

Viable eggs are usually chalk-white in color. A yellowish shell (see single separated egg) may indicate infertility or improper shell calcification.

A light misting sometimes will induce breeding.

After mating, if you choose to do so, you can separate the sexes again. Continue to feed them heavily until your snake regains its pre-hibernation weight and appearance. Several days following the female's next shed, she will deposit her eggs. One breeder in the Pacific Northwest has found his snakes will lay their eggs ten days after that second shed.

The egg "box."

Gestation and Egg Deposition

Gestating snakes need rather warm, secure areas in which to bask, and ultimately, to deposit their eggs (or in the case of *E. rufodorsata* [see page 88], to give birth).

As with all other aspects associated with the keeping of rat snakes, the size of gestation and deposition/incubation sites must be tailored to the needs of your specimens.

The Egg "Box"

An opaque plastic dish partially filled with barely moistened peat or sphagnum will often be accepted as a deposition site. The site becomes even more desirable to the snakes if it is covered, either by an opaque lid or by placing the tub in a darkened cardboard box. In both cases, be sure to cut an appropriately sized access hole. If the cage temperatures are inordinately cold, the deposition tub can be set on top of a heating cable or pad (set on Low) to increase warmth. Remember that heat from beneath will quickly dry the sphagnum (or other medium) and remoistening this will be necessary on a regular basis. (Once the eggs have been laid, take care not to wet them directly when remoistening the medium in the deposition tub.)

Although we prefer to keep the deposition boxes available throughout the year (the snakes use them as hide-boxes during the nonreproductive season), some breeders place the boxes in the cage only during the breeding season. Remember that many snakes will multiple-clutch (lay more than one batch of eggs). Clean the box and replace the sphagnum (or other substrate) after the first deposition, but don't remove the deposition box early.

Behavior of Females

Female rat snakes investigate their cages prior to deposition, looking for

An incubator can be purchased at many feed stores.

Hatchling snakes, such as this amelanistic corn snake, may remain in the egg for a day or more after pipping. Photographed at The Gourmet Rodent.

the best spot in which to lay their eggs. Your female will probably spend some time "resting" in the egg deposition tub before she actually places the eggs there. Some snakes are a little slow to catch on—they'll spend days in the tub, only moving to lay their eggs in the water bowl. To avoid this, remove the water dish, replacing it for only an hour or so each evening.

Feeding

Gravid female rat snakes may cease feeding a week, two, or even three, prior to egg deposition. After egg deposition, offer food to the female. Small meals offered at frequent intervals seem best. Female rat snakes that retain or quickly regain their body weight following egg deposition will breed more frequently and successfully than underweight specimens or females that are slow to recover their weight.

Incubation Procedures/Techniques

With the oviparous rat snakes, you need to provide correct temperatures during gestation and incubation. Incorrect incubation procedures can result in embryo deformity or death.

Incubators can be either homemade or purchased. You can make one from a styrofoam cooler, an inexpensive

thermostat from a hardware or livestock feed store, a length of heating cable, and a few feet of electrical wire. If you prefer, any electrician can assemble one for a fee. Chick-egg incubators from any feed store are big enough for several clutches of rat snakes and can be used year after year.

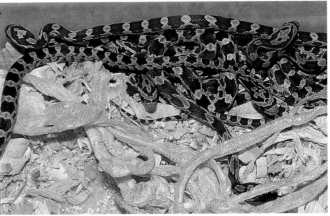

Within a few days after emerging from their eggs, baby snakes undergo a "postnatal shed." The shed skins of this clutch of corn snakes are clearly visible. Photographed at The Gourmet Rodent.

Babies take their time emerging from the egg.

Temperature: The suggested incubation temperature is between 76 and 82°F (24–28°C), see species accounts, beginning on page 43, for details. Some slight variation of temperature may be desirable during incubation. Incubation humidity should be maintained at 80–95 percent. We keep an open container of water in the incubator. Keep the incubator dark. Once laid, eggs can be gently moved but must not be turned. Frequent handling, rough handling, and excessively brilliant lighting are not good for the developing embryos.

Hatching: In nearly all cases, healthy full-term young will emerge from their eggs or egg membrane without incident. They will slit the egg with the help of an egg tooth on their upper lip, and will emerge within a day or two, peering out at intervals. In rare cases (such as when the egg membrane dries too quickly due to improper humidity), the babies may need a little help escaping. Raising the relative humidity often seems to help the most. A short slit in the top of the egg or egg membrane may also help. Take care not to cut

blood vessels. Caution: If you slit an egg prematurely (sometimes by only a few days) it can be fatal to the baby.

Sexing Your Rat Snake

"Probing," as shown in the illustration below, is the most reliable method of sexing subadult and adult rat snakes. When gently inserted into the hemipenial pocket of a male, a lubricated probe will slide smoothly back seven to twelve subcaudal scale lengths. If the snake is a female, the probe will only insert from two to four subcaudal scale lengths. If the probe is of incorrect diameter or is forced, injury to the snake may occur. Hatchling rat snakes may be sexed by manually everting the hemipenes of males. This is done by placing the thumb a few scales posterior to the vent and rolling the thumb firmly, but very gently, forward. Females, of course, have no hemipenes to evert. Both sexing and manual eversion of the hemipenes is best learned from an experienced hobbyist.

Experience will also help you sex adult snakes just by comparing the shape and length of the tail. To accommodate the hemipenes, the tail of a male is broader at the base than that of a similarly sized female. Also, the tail of the male usually tapers less abruptly and is comparatively longer.

7–12 Scales

Male
Tail long and tapering

2–4 Scales

Female
Tail short and abruptly tapered

Species Accounts: The New World Rat Snakes

Meet the Corn Snake

Where Corns Are Found

The corn snake, *E. g. guttata*, is found over an immense area in the United States. It may be found in a variety of habitats (a snake that is able to successfully utilize a variety of habitats is called a *habitat generalist*) from southeastern New Jersey to the southernmost tip of the Florida Keys, and from those states west to central Kentucky and eastern Louisiana. An area of intergradation with the more westerly race, the Great Plains rat snake, occurs in northwestern Louisiana, southcentral Arkansas, and extreme eastern Texas. Occasionally, natural hybrids with black rat snake complex animals are found.

Colors of Corns

The brightest: The most brightly colored corn snakes seem to occur in the central Atlantic states, and those on both the northern and southern peripheries of the range tend to be smaller than the corn snakes from the interior areas. The ground color may vary from orangeish (the "normal" phase) to gray (southern Florida) to brownish (a rare phase in southwestern Florida); however, west of the Mississippi, the corn snakes (again rather uniformly) assume a darker, drabber hue, and are called the Great Plains rat snake (the old, outdated name is Emory's rat snake), or *Elaphe guttata emoryi*.

"Normal": What is "normal"? Throughout our discussion of the corn snake, *Elaphe g. guttata*, you will see periodic mention of the term "normal." The term refers to the coloration of the usual wild-caught specimen, and this varies somewhat geographically. The basic corn snake is a dull orange snake with (often narrowly outlined) black-edged red dorsal and lateral blotches. The venter is prominently checkered with black and white. Hatchlings are less colorful than adults.

Today, corn snakes are captive-bred in large numbers, but there was a time, just a few decades ago, when,

Anerythristic corn snakes are rather commonly found in southwestern Florida.

The "Okeetee phase" of the normal, wild corn snake is typified by a great intensity of color. The color of this young adult will brighten with age.

if a hobbyist wanted a corn snake, that hobbyist would have to either purchase a wild-collected specimen or go out and collect one.

First Personal Sightings

During the 1950s, one of the author's friends, a teacher who had an inordi-

Road hunting at night can sometimes yield surprises.

nate interest in snakes, purchased a corn snake from the now long-defunct Ross Allen's Reptile Institute. When the snake was taken out of the bag, the author could hardly believe his eyes. Was it possible that there could be a snake so brilliantly colored? Indeed it was, and although it took a few additional years, he eventually got to meet this species in the field.

By this time, Gordon Johnston and the author were so interested in snakes that they made jaunts back and forth across the country to see them in their natural habitat and to try to learn more about them.

One of the first "exotics" they sought was a corn snake. The range of the corns includes southern New Jersey, and they made several trips in search of those red serpents—all to no avail. Finding a corn snake in the field became almost an obsession. They eventually succeeded, but only after traveling much farther than southern New Jersey. So, one Easter school vacation (more than four decades ago), they set off for Okeetee, South Carolina, where the corn snakes were said to be common and extraordinarily pretty.

At that time, Okeetee was barely known, and it was studded with dozens of abandoned, decrepit houses and barns, piles of rusted roofing tins, and old stoves.

The duo looked through a few piles of tin and found nothing of note. That wasn't really surprising—snakes can be very hard to find, even when a concerted search is being made. At one stopping place, the author turned over a sheet of tin. There, against the pine straw lay a snake with bright scarlet saddles, broadly edged with jet black, set against a vibrant red-orange ground color. Over the years the author has seen many corns in the field, but only one has left a memory as strong as that first Okeetee corn.

The second corn was a hatchling, barely more than shoestring size, remarkable because it was an albino, spotted while traveling late one night at 65 mph (104 km) on a heavily trafficked road in west central Florida. We were headed for the field with two friends, to hunt up and photograph some of Florida's more uncommon bromeliads and orchids. Snakes were not foremost on our minds. Suddenly, we thought we saw a small snake, maybe a scarlet king, on the center stripe of the road. After edging the car out of traffic, the author hopped out and ran back along the road, flashlight sweeping the edge of the road. Suddenly, there was a tiny snake just off the road—but it wasn't a scarlet kingsnake; it was a corn snake—an *albino* corn snake.

That little snake proved to be a male that sired a dynasty of albino corns, but there are now literally dozens of normal and "designer" color morphs of the corn snake available either from private breeders or from pet stores. Let's look at both natural and created corn snake morphs.

The Color Morphs

The Miami phase corn, with its maroon on pearl gray theme, is a familiar sight in much of the southern third of the Florida peninsula. This amazingly resilient snake persists in some areas of downtown Miami.

The rosy rat snake is found to the south of the Florida mainland, in the Florida Keys. This is a much sought, somewhat smaller, color morph of the corn snake. These are paler corn snakes, with reduced black pigment. Once designated as *Elaphe guttata rosacea*, the Keys corns are now thought to be merely a variant of the red rat snake and the subspecific designator of *rosacea* has been dropped.

All of the corn snakes of the Florida Keys were once designated as rosies,

The term "rosy rat snake" is applied to the somewhat pallid corn snakes of the Lower Florida Keys.

but the term is most readily applied to those furthest removed from the influences of the Florida mainland (those of the Lower Keys). These show very reduced amounts of black in their patterns but reduced black is also known from some corn snake populations on the Florida mainland. Many specimens from Hillsborough and Pinellas counties (the Tampa Bay area) are as rosy as those from the Lower Keys.

The corn snakes of the Lower Keys have a reputation for being difficult to find, perhaps even rare. We have not found this to be so. A few years ago we were on one of the Lower Keys and saw a half dozen corns in two nights. A more recent photographic venture in that area brought a couple of vibrant corns without even consciously searching for them, beneath some railroad ties in a field on Key West. The Keys corn populations may be very secretive rather than actually rare. (Lower Keys populations of the corn snake are protected in Florida.)

The blood-red, a particularly bright corn, was found near Gainesville, Florida. It lacks the darker saddles. Hatchlings are not particularly impressive. The ground color is fairly light and the blotches are much better defined that they will be when the snakes are

Randi Sherman's adult "snow corn" is a magnificent specimen.

adult; however, the black of the venter and the lateral blotches are both noticeably reduced. The venter of this morph is often nearly as red as the dorsum but may be patterned with diffuse blotches of white. The black that normally outlines the dorsal saddles is entirely lacking. (This color morph has proven to be difficult to keep. If you are considering a purchase of this morph, be sure that you insist on feeding specimens.)

Bill Brant (The Gourmet Rodent) developed the "Christmas corn snake." Dark green, rather than black, outlines the dorsal saddles.

Other Morphs

Other morphs include the sunglow (a reddish amelanistic), and an amelanistic Okeetee corn (black dorsal markings replaced with white).

Candycane corn snakes are typified by precisely outlined, deep red to red-orange blotching against a paler than normal ground color. The overall appearance is quite pretty.

Snow corns have a pearl white ground color and the pearl white centered dorsal blotches are precise but faded and pale. With increasing age, a wash of yellow, orange, pink, or green may develop. If present, this suffusion of color will be brightest anteriolaterally.

The ghost corn exhibits hypomelanistic (reduced melanin) anerythristics (without red pigment), being an almost translucent pink at hatching and turning pinkish-lavender with growth.

The blizzard corn is a further refinement of the snow corn but the pattern of the blizzard corn is all but invisible. In essence, this is a white snake with bright ruby eyes.

Hypomelanistic corn snakes are red on orange with a few dark highlights. Their dorsal pattern is an irregular lineate marking, called a zigzag, or zipper. The normally wide dorsal blotches are somewhat reduced in width and many are connected by a thinner, irregular middorsal line. This pattern may be present in amelanistic (albino), normal (red), or anerythristic (black) corn snakes. Because some black remains on these anerythristic specimens, the dorsal and lateral blotches are faintly but precisely defined.

A "motley" corn morph may bear partial striping, H or ladder-like blotch connections, and the saddles may be as wide as the light pigment between them or they may virtually dominate the snake. Whether wide or narrow, large or small, the blotches are best defined middorsally and meld (at times almost imperceptibly) with the yellowish lateral coloration. If present at all, the lateral blotches and ventral pattern are greatly reduced. The pattern also occurs on albino (amelanistic) mutants.

The recessive striped trait, like the motley trait, reduces belly patterns; however, unlike the irregular dorsal patterns of motley corns, the striped corn snakes bear well-defined, complete or broken, dorsal stripes, and broken, longitudinal, lateral striping. The stripes may be of regular or irregular thickness. Striping has been developed in normal red corns as well as in the anerythristic, amelanistic, and even more complex mutants.

The Christmas corn snake mutant has rather dull hatchlings, giving little indication of the pale greens and crimsons that will develop with age. This mutation is the result of selectively breeding certain insular South Carolina corn snakes.

Creamsicle is the name given the amelanistic intergrade between the corn snake and its western race, the Great Plains rat snake, *E. g. emoryi*. While the normal intergrade produces a snake that typically is brighter than the Great Plains but duller than the corn snake, when the mutation for

"Red albino" corn snakes are beautiful and plentiful in the pet trade.

amelanism is factored in, the offspring produced have a beautiful yellow-white ground color and peach to pale orange blotches. The color intensity of these magnificent intergrades intensifies with advancing age.

Finding a Corn Snake in the Wild

Over their range, corn snake populations may vary from rare (often on the peripheries of the range) to common, or actually abundant. They, and all other herpetofauna, are protected

Striped "albino" corn snakes are pretty and popular. This baby was hatched at Glades Herp.

The "creamsicle corn snake" has resulted from selective intergrading between the corn and the Great-Plains rat snakes. Photo taken at Glades Herp.

Bill Love (Glades Herp) bred and photographed this beautiful "albino motley" corn snake.

turn debris (especially roofing tins or other such cover in the early spring—but be careful! Venomous snakes also seek such cover. If you *do* come across a venomous snake species, carefully replace the tin, or whatever, move a short distance away, and resume searching). When the weather is warm, slowly drive old country roads in the early evening. Corn snakes often cross these. Again, be certain you know what you are picking up before you pick it up as corns are not the only snakes that cross roadways.

Remember that corns are bred in huge numbers and in a variety of colors, so it is no longer necessary for you to collect a corn to have one. Practice conservation—find, watch, and photograph—but leave the animal in its habitat for others to also sight and enjoy.

by some states, but may be legally collected in others.

"Fielding" To find a corn snake, go to where the snakes are—the edges of old agricultural fields (corn and soybean are favored, hence the name "corn snakes"), woodland edges (especially those where litter is strewn about), or even urban areas where some cover remains. Walk slowly along the field and woodland edges,

Turning debris is another way to find snakes.

Keeping and Breeding the Corn Snake

Feeding: As adults, captive corn snakes thrive on rodent prey. Most hatchlings and virtually all juveniles do likewise. In the wild, hatchling corn snakes are as apt to feed on amphibians and small lizards as on rodents. An occasional hatchling (even from multiple-generation captives) may insist on lizards or tree frogs at the beginning. These holdouts can usually be switched to pinky mice within a few meals by scenting the pinky with the preferred prey species. Scent the pinky less with each feeding, then desist entirely.

Size and behavior: The moderate size (commonly to 4.5 feet [1.3 m], rarely to 6 feet [1.8 m], the official record) and inordinate tractability of corn snakes make them an ideal species for even novice keepers. The "designer colors" now available, and the possibility (even probability) that a new color or pattern will appear in any clutch of hatchlings, tends to hold the interest of even long-time hobbyists.

Eggs: Corns may produce from six to about 20 eggs. More than one clutch may be laid annually. Smaller and younger females tend to lay smaller clutches than older and larger females.

Brumation: This is not necessary to breed most corn snakes. If you choose to brumate your corn snake, a temperature between 45°F and 52°F (7–11°C) for a period of 90 days is satisfactory. Some breeders retain their snakes in total darkness during hibernation; others allow a natural, unenhanced photoperiod.

We do not truly brumate our corn snake breeders. Rather, we allow winter (December, January, and February) temperatures to drop by a few degrees during the day and a few more at night, and we allow an entirely natural photoperiod. The breeders continue to eat, but meal size and feeding frequency is also reduced. Water is always available. With such a regimen, corn snakes cycle reproductively and breed readily.

The Great Plains Rat Snake

The least colorful of the natural members of the corn snake complex is

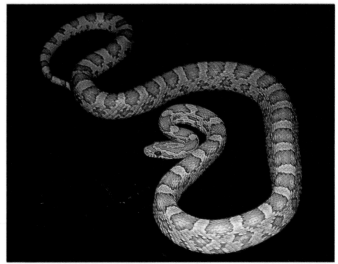

"Ghost corns" retain more pattern than "snow corns." This specimen was photographed at The Gourmet Rodent.

the wide-ranging Great Plains rat snake of our central states and northeastern Mexico. (Although we have included it as a corn snake group member, some taxonomists consider this snake a full species, *E. emoryi*.) This abundant and interesting serpent

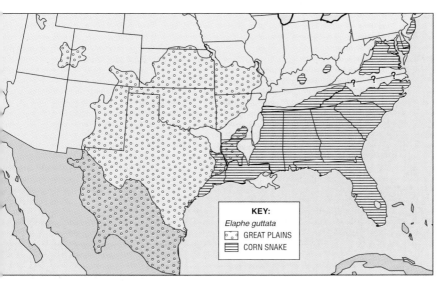

KEY:

Elaphe guttata

GREAT PLAINS

CORN SNAKE

49

is a pleasing combination of gray on gray.

We have most frequently encountered these serpents on Texas roadways. At times, when nothing else seems to be crossing, Great Plains rat snakes will be actively crossing roads in some numbers. Despite its somewhat dull color (most Great Plains rat snakes are less contrastingly colored than anerythristic corn snakes), it is always a pleasure to happen across these creatures. Great Plains rat snakes seldom exceed 4.5 feet (1.35 m) in length and the record length is only 5 feet one quarter inch (1.53 m).

Color morphs: Because Great Plains rat snakes are so dull when compared to the more easterly corn snake, not many hobbyists seek them out. Of the commonly seen "designer corns," the Great Plains rat snake has contributed its genes to the creamsicle corn (see page 47). Albino Great Plains rat snakes have been found, but most of those now seen in captivity have albino corn snake genes somewhere in their background.

Hibernation: Since most Great Plains rat snakes originate from cooler

Check the roadside trees at night for Obsoleta.

areas than corn snakes, a period of actual hibernation may be required to cycle them for breeding. A reduction in winter temperature (45–52°F [7–11°C]) and a photoperiod for a period of 70 to 90 days is recommended.

The Black Rat Snake and Its Subspecies—Blacks, Yellows, and Relatives

These can be considered American rat snakes, being essentially restricted to eastern North America, between Canada and Mexico. (The exception is a small population of the black rat snake in Canada on the eastern end of Lake Ontario.)

For beginners: From the standpoint of hardiness, the several members of this group are ideal starter snakes. They do well either with or without a period of winter dormancy, although those from northern areas seem to need winter dormancy for reproduction. Most feed readily year round if kept warm. Captive breeding supplies most of the specimens available in the pet market, which lessens the number of specimens taken from the wild. Captive breeding has resulted in albino (amelanistic) or other designer morphs.

Catch your own: If you live in or visit the eastern United States, you can usually catch your own *obsoleta*. They are common in the usual rat snake habitat of litter in open fields, rocky ledges, or sunning on tree trunks. The only drawback to catching your own is that the adults are large and impressive, and all subspecies will bite if/when they feel threatened. Most tame with gentle handling.

Five subspecies of *obsoleta* are currently recognized: the black rat snake, *E. o. obsoleta*; the yellow rat snake, *E. o. quadrivittata*; the Everglades rat snake, *E. o. rossalleni*; the gray rat snake, *E. o. spiloides*; and the Texas rat snake, *E. o. lindheimeri*. Additionally at least four easily distinguishable intergrades (three of which were once themselves considered subspecies) are known: the Gulf Hammock variant, *E. o. spiloides* x *E. o. quadrivittata* (once designated as *E. o. williamsi*), the Keys variant (a dark orange-brown, striped, and blotched creature formerly called *E. o. deckerti*); and the dusky, dark-striped narrow blotched morph from the Outer Banks of North Carolina that was once called *E. o. parallela* (the common name of this drab beast was the Outer Banks rat snake). The black rat-yellow rat intergrade from the Carolinas and elsewhere, where the ranges of the two races abut, is often referred to as the greenish rat snake.

Tree-dwellers: *Obsoleta* complex snakes are largely arboreal but can be found in roadside dumps or amid other human debris. In certain areas of Florida, yellow and gray rat snakes, their intergrades, and corn snakes can be found by shining a strong flashlight beam upward into roadside or canalside trees after dark. In the past, yellows, corns, and Everglades rat snakes were abundant in pumphouses that controlled crop irrigation, despite the all-pervasive smell of diesel fumes.

Tires: Another, lesser-known method of searching for rat snakes in southern Florida has essentially ended. This involved overgrown roadsides and the blown-out automobile inner tubes found there. For those who don't remember inner tubes, these were the air-retaining predecessors of tubeless tires. In a blow-out, the tire would separate from the wheel hub and the now airless inner tube would slap its way free, eventually coming to rest on a weedy roadside. The inner tubes were black, a color that warmed up quickly even on the coolest of days. Somehow, the rat snakes learned that those blown-out pieces of sun-warmed tire were good places to thermoregulate on cool days. By walking the

shoulders and checking the tubes, you could often find a fair number of rat snakes—sometimes more than one in a tube! It was a non-demanding way to hunt, soon to be remembered only by old-time herpers.

Obsoleta Subspecies and Intergrades

The members of the obsoleta complex rat snakes are of such interest that we will discuss each separately. Some are favorites of both American and European hobbyists, and recently, Asian enthusiasts as well.

Reproduction: Both the size and age of the snake combine to determine sexual maturity. All the *obsoleta* are oviparous and, if fed heavily most can attain sexual maturity in their second summer. Even slow growers usually are sexually mature by their third year of life. Females of 3 feet (0.9 m) in length can successfully breed and produce fair-sized clutches of eggs. A 32-inch-long (81 cm) female yellow rat snake (which was actually slender for her size) produced five viable eggs. Small and young specimens have fewer and smaller eggs than older, larger adults. The clutch of an old, healthy female (anywhere from four years of age and up) often numbers 25 or more eggs. The eggs are easily incubated (suggested temperature, 82–86°F [28–30°C]) and hatch in 60 days. The hatchling snakes are robust and easily reared. Hatchlings can exceed a foot (30 cm) in length, and some 16 inches (40 cm) long have been reported.

The Black Rat Snake

The black rat snake, *E. o. obsoleta*, is the largest of the several subspecies and, with a record size of 101 inches (2.56 m), is one of the largest snakes in America. The specific name means *dim*, probably referring to the snake's subdued coloration.

Range: The black snake is the northeasternmost member of the group. It ranges from the southern tip of Ontario, southern Massachusetts, and southeastern Minnesota, southward to northern Louisiana and central Georgia. It is largely absent from the coastal plain of the Carolinas where it is replaced by the smaller but more brightly colored yellow rat snake.

Not wholly black: Even though normally a dark color and hence less visually appealing than a brighter snake, the black rat snake is a favorite of many beginning reptile enthusiasts. It is common, impressive, and hardy. At least two genetically distinct albino forms are available, and to make things even more complex, a fair number of intergrades between albino black rats and other races are now available to hobbyists under names

Bruce Morgan is the owner of many infrequently seen rat snake hybrids. This specimen is a hybrid between a black rat and a corn snake.

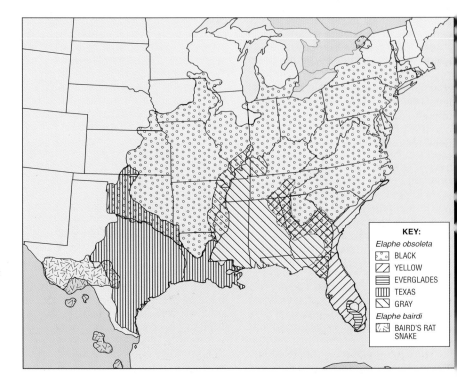

KEY:

Elaphe obsoleta
- BLACK
- YELLOW
- EVERGLADES
- TEXAS
- GRAY

Elaphe bairdi
- BAIRD'S RAT SNAKE

that may, or may not, reflect their lineage. The normal coloration of the black rat snake varies considerably over its wide range. The darkest (blackest) individuals seem to come from the Northeast and the mountains of the Southeast. Specimens that we have found in the southern Blue Ridge Mountains have been every bit as dark as specimens we have found in the Berkshires of Massachusetts. On the other hand, black rat snakes from the western part of the range are often more brown than black. The largest individuals tend to be the darkest. Under bright light, the dark blotches of babyhood can still be seen on most. It is the light ground color that becomes suffused with melanin, finally obscuring the dorsal blotching. The interstitial skin is often lighter, being white or reddish, and the throat is light (often white). The light gular coloration may extend for a variable distance onto the venter.

The two albino morphs: These differ dramatically from each other. One is a mostly white snake with reddish saddles and red eyes. The other is much redder, often being lavender to pale red with brilliant strawberry dorsal saddles. Interestingly, different genetic factors determine the color abnormalities of these two snakes. Thus, when the two are bred together (to the surprise of most breeders), the resulting offspring are of the normal, pigmented coloration.

A "brindle" variant: This variant, having variably reduced melanin (hypomelanism), is now also available. In color, this form may vary from a light tannish-pink with reddish blotches (brightest and best defined anteriorly), to a rather uniformly patterned graybrown on dirty tan. These snakes may not be particularly pretty, but they are very different!

The albino bubblegum rat snake: This is a very pretty snake with a combined lineage of Everglades, yellow, and black rat snakes. With growth, the babies develop pink blotches on an almost white ground color, with variable highlights of yellow or pale orange. The ads for these claim that "no two are identical."

The Yellow Rat Snake

The subspecific name of the yellow rat snake, *E. o. quadrivittata*, refers to the four rather prominent lines borne by adult specimens. The common name refers, of course, to the ground color of the adults. Like all complex members (except the Everglades rat snakes, which are light in color), juvenile yellow rat snakes are quite dark, having a gray ground color and nearly black saddles.

Range and color: Ground coloration on yellow rats may vary considerably. Those on the northern and western peripheries of their range tend to be a duller yellow than specimens from the coast and the southern portions. The range of yellow rat snakes extends southward along the coastal plain from just south of North

Albinism in black rat snakes is attributed to at least two separate, non-compatible, characteristics. Thus, the breeding of two albino black rat snakes may produce all normally colored babies.

The bulge in its body indicates that this yellow rat snake, found in Alachua County, Florida, has recently fed.

Carolina's Albemarle Peninsula to the central Florida Keys. The most intensely colored specimens occur on the extreme south of peninsular Florida to the region of Big Pine Key.

Over most of its range, the yellow rat snake retains its own subspecific integrity. This, the second largest of the *obsoleta* rat snakes, is known to occasionally exceed 7 feet (2.1 cm) in length. The ground color varies from straw to rather bright yellow and the stripes can be broad or narrow, and dark, or rather poorly defined. The adults in some populations retain vestiges of the juvenile saddles and in some areas (Cape Coral, Florida, for one) adults retain well-defined saddles and lack stripes.

Albino yellow rat snakes have been collected and are being bred. These specimens retain the saddles; the stripes are poorly defined.

Intergrades: The greenish rat snake is a naturally occurring intergrade between the yellow and the black rat snakes. It is common where the ranges of the two subspecies abut in areas of Georgia, extreme southern

South Carolina, and on northward to southeastern Tennessee. Often a dingy olive color when adult, the four stripes are usually prominent.

The Gulf Hammock variant of northwestern peninsular Florida is also a naturally occurring intergrade between the gray rat and the yellow rat snakes. A grayish ground color, this variant retains the juvenile saddles and develops the usual yellow rat four stripes.

Of the naturally occurring rat snake variants, the Keys or Deckert's rat snake is the most attractive. Like the Gulf Hammock animal, the Keys variant retains the juvenile saddles and develops stripes. However, its ground color is yellow-orange, deep orange, or brownish-orange, and the tongue is black. The saddles can be prominent or vague and brownish to maroon in color. The prettiest animals are those with the deep orange ground color and maroon saddles. Apparently, this snake has never been common. Today, a Keys variant rat snake is considered much harder to find than the rosy rat variant of the corn snake (see page 45).

The Everglades rat snake is our favorite *obsoleta.* These big orange snakes with obscure striping were once a recognized presence in the herpetofauna of inland Florida south of Lake Okeechobee. This was back in the days when the Army Corps of Engineers, the sugarcane industry, and sod farms were still trying to determine the most effective and cheapest way to devastate the Everglades. Back then (more than four decades ago), a drive from Clewiston to Andytown (the latter town now buried beneath a maze of Interstate Highways) down U.S. Route 27 revealed only the Everglades and seas of waving sawgrass stretched to both the western and eastern horizons. Sometimes the grass was dry, sometimes, after the passing of a tropical storm, the sedges would stand in a foot or more of water. Hammocks of tropical vegetation stood high, dry, and isolated from each other by vast expanses of sawgrass. It was in this habitat that the Everglades rat snake evolved. Glades rat snakes can exceed 6 feet (1.8 m) in total length. At that size they are definitely impressive. The body, head, chin, and eyes are an (often rich) orange. The tongue is entirely red. (Black tongue pigment would indicate a "visiting" yellow rat snake in the fairly recent lineage.)

Changing populations: Newcomers to the herpetocultural field are unfamiliar with the intensity and suite of color characteristics once found in the rat snakes along Route 27 in south Florida, but we remember well the Everglades rat snakes. In those days, before the 1970s, true yellow rats, with their paler ground color, better defined stripes, white chins, and black tongues were uncommon enough south of Clewiston to evoke comment when one was found. Several years after the sod and sugarcane fields began production (in other words, the "draining of the Everglades"), we were finding as many yellow as Everglades rat snakes along that same stretch of road. Today, 99 percent of the rat snakes found along Route 27 will have virtually no Everglades characteristics. This is probably because the draining of the Glades allowed the yellow rat snakes to continue their move southward, genetically swamping their Everglades cousins. Thus, with every succeeding generation, the defining characteristics of the Everglades rat snake were further diluted. Today, except for the possibility of a few isolated specimens that retain some of the characteristics, wild Everglades rat snakes are as much a memory as the Glades themselves.

Captive breeding successes: Does this mean that Everglades

rat snakes are gone entirely? Fortunately, no. Through selective breeding, herpetoculturists have kept this race alive and well, perhaps even enhanced. Not only are Everglades rat snakes produced each year, but a hypomelanistic phase has been developed. With the reduction of the melanin, the body color of these adults is a resplendent red-orange. This snake looks more like what we think an albino ought to look like than the albinos themselves do.

Other morphs: Another project involving Everglades snakes has produced a recessive blotchless phase. Not even the hatchlings have the normal dorsal blotches. Other striped subspecies have been worked in here and the phase is now available in normally pigmented and amelanistic morphs.

The Gray Rat Snake

Very little line breeding or other genetic enhancement has been done by breeders with the gray rat snake, *E. o. spiloides*. The gray rat snake is the deep south's lighter colored version of the north's black rat snake. Actually, there are two color phases of the gray rat snake—the rather dark, gray on gray "normal phase," and the lighter, prettier gray on grayish-white

Bill Love (Glades Herp) has been developing interesting phases of the Everglades rat snake. He photographed this hypomelanistic specimen.

Hatchlings of three races of Elaphe obsoleta *are shown here. The black rat snake is the darkest, the yellow rat snake the next lighter, and the Everglades rat snake the lightest.*

"Them" was a normally pigmented, but dicephalic (two-headed) Texas rat snake owned by Glades Herp.

"white-oak phase." The dark dorsal saddles (which this subspecies retains throughout its life and to which the subspecific name of *spiloides,* spotted, pertains) of the normal phase are often bordered with an even darker, narrow edging. Those of the white oak phase are often narrowly edged with a very light gray. The saddles may be completely dark or light-centered. Gray rats retain the blotches of babyhood.

Tree-dwellers: Gray rats are persistently arboreal. Although we have caught many crossing sparsely trav-

eled roadways, many have been seen high in trees and in the rafters of deserted buildings. The biggest recorded gray rat was 84.25 inches (2.13 m).

Range: Gray rat snakes may be encountered from coastal Panhandle Florida to western Mississippi. From there they range northward to northern Alabama and the somewhat warmer Mississippi River valley to extreme western Kentucky, southeastern Illinois, and immediately adjacent Indiana.

The black rat snake is one of the most widely spread and frequently encountered rat snakes.

Wild Everglades rat snakes are now difficult to find. This is a captive-bred specimen.

The Texas Rat Snake

If you are enthralled by belligerence in a snake, let us introduce you to the Texas (or Lindheimer's) rat snake, *E. o. lindhiemeri*, named for herpetologist Fred Lindheimer. There may be no other harmless snake in America quite so ready to bite.

Color: The Texas rat snake is another of the subspecies that retains the blotches throughout its life. In coloration, most Texas rats are lighter than a black rat and darker than a gray rat. The ground color can vary from straw-yellow to orange, but more usually tan or light brown. The dorsal blotches are rather elongate, fairly narrow, and medium to deep brown, either with or without light centers. The contrast between the dark dorsal blotches and the lighter ground color is not very great. The lateral interstitial skin can vary from yellow to orange. The interstitial color may spill over onto the leading edges of some lateral scales, but since the trailing edge of the preceding scales overlaps, the little brilliance may not be seen unless the snake is distended with food or tightly coiled.

Other morphs: Actually, few hobbyists work with normal, wild-caught Texas rat snakes; however, many do keep and breed two of the most common mutants—an albino (actually amelanistic rather than a true albino), and a leucistic (see Glossary, page 100). Of the two, the albino is the less pretty, being white (almost translucent when hatched) with pink saddles. The colors intensify somewhat with increasing age. The dorsal saddles of older adults are usually pale strawberry. The eyes of the amelanistic are pink.

The leucistic morph is a beautiful creature. It is a solid, unpatterned white and has gray-blue eyes.

The Baird's Rat Snake

Baird's rat snake is another of the species frequently found by accident.

Although it may pale with advancing age, this Keys variant yellow rat snake owned by Bruce Morgan is one of the prettiest we have seen.

Pretty in its own quiet way, the gray rat snake is not eagerly sought by collectors.

Although albinism is now known in Texas rat snakes, the stark white examples are leucistic, rather than albinistic. Photographed at Glades Herp.

Specimens of E. bairdi *found in Texas are usually grayer than this Mexican example.*

As a matter of fact, the author saw his first specimen some thirty years ago while looking for gray-banded kingsnakes and Trans-Pecos rat snakes in west Texas. The second specimen wasn't seen until 1993, when he was again in Texas, looking for herps, and the third was a very unexpected bonus, seen the next evening only a hundred yards from that first specimen three decades earlier.

Appearance: Although the colors of the moderately sized Baird's rat snake are muted, these are a pretty, easily handled, and very hardy rat snake. Dorsally, adult Baird's rat snakes may vary from a dusty pearl gray through a powdery orange-brown to a rather warm burnt orange. Adult males are usually suffused with more and brighter orange than females. Adults have four dark to orangeish stripes of variable intensity and contrast. The pair of dorsolateral stripes are usually the better defined. The brighter specimens (especially those with orange striping) seem to come from the southernmost part of the range (the Mexican states of Nuevo Leon and Tamaulipas). The interstitial skin and often the anterior edge of each scale may be a rather bright orange. The entire snake may have orangish overtones, brighter anteriorly. The venter is usually an unpatterned yellow to orange. Hatchlings and juveniles are grayish with a busy pattern of many thin dorsal saddles. Lateral blotches are also numerous and rather well-defined. A curved dark bar crosses the snout immediately anterior to the eyes and a dark postocular stripe runs from eye to mouth. With growth, both markings pale and eventually disappear completely. The head of an adult Baird's rat snake is entirely without markings.

Baird's rat snake (the name honors Spencer Fullerton Baird, a nineteenth-century vertebrate zoologist) was originally considered a subspecies of the very wide ranging *E. obsoleta*. It is a moderately heavy-bodied snake with a maximum size of just over five feet (1.5 m). Females are generally longer than the males; the males are usually more orange than the females. Two color morphs, the Mexican and Texas, are now being bred by hobbyists. The Mexican differs from the Texas specimens by a gray head and a ground color suffused with orange. Now that some interest is being shown in them, these once rather expensive snakes are now being seen with increasing frequency, and at lower prices.

Reproduction: Although these snakes seem to reproduce best if hibernated, our pairs produced viable eggs with little more than a slight winter cooling and a reduction of photoperiod. Hatchlings are about a foot in length. Clutches number from four to ten eggs. Incubation nears 90 days at 82–86°F (28–29°C). The hatchlings almost always feed readily on newly born mice. Large, healthy females often produce two clutches annually.

The Two Fox Snakes

Until recently, the two fox snakes, the eastern and the western, were grouped as *Elaphe vulpina* subspecies. Today they are considered two full species: the western fox snake, *E. vulpina*, and the eastern fox snake, *E. gloydi*. This separation seems a reasonable approach, for at no point are the ranges of the two contiguous, nor do the two naturally intergrade.

The fox snakes have probably derived both their common and scientific name of *vulpina* from the scent of the musk produced by the anal glands. To some the odor is reminiscent of the red fox; in all cases it is a musky odor best avoided by not frightening the snakes.

Reluctant feeders: Although they are quite pretty, neither of the fox snakes is popular as a captive. Like many northern latitude snake species, fox snakes taken from the wild (especially in the fall as they near hibernation) can be problematic feeders. This reluctance to feed is natural for snakes in the wild, as they would soon be entering hibernacula (see Glossary, page 100). In captivity, subjected to warm temperatures and continued activity, these snakes can lose a fair amount of body weight before they are again ready (both physiologically and psychologically) to feed.

Coloration: Despite being from different areas, the two fox snakes are difficult to distinguish if the origin of the specimen is not known. The ground color of both tends toward straw yellow, and the dorsal and lateral blotches (an average of 41 between nape and tail on *E. vulpina* and 34 on *E. gloydi*) are dark. The head of the adults of both species can be orange to coppery-red, although *E. gloydi* is more apt to be the brighter. Quite unfortunately, the reddish head often leads to the fox snakes being mistaken for a copperhead and summarily dispatched. The fact that these snakes nervously vibrate their tails in the leaves when approached leads to an alternate erroneous identification. Hearing the "whirr," these big constrictors are also often mistakenly identified as rattlesnakes.

The juveniles of both tend to have a paler ground color than the adults and also have the blotches edged in black or darker brown. A head pattern is usually discernible, the most prominent markings being a transverse bar between the eyes and a dark postocular stripe that angles downward to the angle of the jaw. The head markings fade to obscurity with advancing age.

Ranges: The western fox snake is found over a fairly extensive range. It occurs in agricultural areas, marshes, and open woodlands from the western portion of Michigan's Upper Peninsula southward along the western and southern shores of Lake Michigan to Illinois and northwestern Indiana, and from there westward in complex fingers of range to southwestern Minnesota, southeastern South Dakota, and eastern Nebraska. It barely enters Missouri in the extreme northwest and again in the extreme northeast and a tiny portion of the eastern central prairieland.

The eastern fox snake is far more circumscribed in range. This species can be encountered in suitable (but

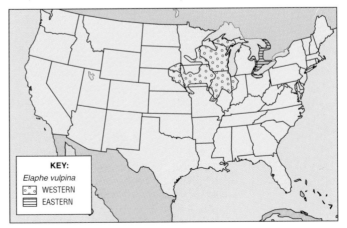

KEY:
Elaphe vulpina
WESTERN
EASTERN

Fox snakes can be difficult to acclimate, but once feeding are hardy. This is an eastern fox snake, E. gloydi.

The Trans-Pecos and Baja Rat Snakes

This rather new genus contains two species of rat snakes that are both best described as slender, big-headed, and "bug-eyed." Both were long considered members of the genus *Elaphe*, but taxonomists felt their divergence sufficiently great for a separate genus, *Bogertophis*. The generic name commemorates the contributions to herpetology by the late Charles M. Bogert.

The two species contained in this genus are *B. subocularis*, the coveted Trans-Pecos rat snake (two subspecies, both referred to as "subocs," for suboculars, by hobbyists). The second species is the poorly known Baja California rat snake, *B. rosaliae*, which is often called the Santa Rosalia rat snake.

Extra row of scales: Both of these snakes share a characteristic unknown in other North American rat snakes. They bear an extra row of scales that separate the eye from the upper lip scales. Called suboculars, it is from these scales that the Trans-Pecos rat snake derives its scientific name. As one might expect after observing the proportionately large eyes, these snakes are primarily nocturnal. They may be encountered as they cross roadways or forage among canyonside boulders, from a few minutes after nightfall until the early hours of the next morning. Rather than being rare, it is their nocturnal habits that keep these secretive desert-dwellers safe from most snake-seekers. On a rainy August night a few years ago, we found seven small Trans-Pecos rat snakes crossing roads within a two hour period.

These are warmth-loving arid climate snakes that fare poorly as captives in areas of high humidity (such as on our southeastern coastal plain or in areas known for fog). Where both

ever-dwindling) patches of habitat along the shores of Lake Huron as well as the western and northern shores of Lake Erie. Less of a habitat generalist than the western fox snake, the eastern species seeks marshlands and open woodland edges associated with marshes. Because of this restricted habitat, the eastern fox snake is considered an imperiled species by most researchers.

Captive behavior: Most of the few fox snakes that enter the pet trade are wild-collected specimens of the western species. Newly collected fox snakes may strike and bite savagely, but quiet with gentle handling. Try to acquire your specimens in the spring, when they are more apt to feed.

Once acclimated and feeding, fox snakes can make interesting, long-lived captives. Adult size is about four feet (1.2 m) in length. Occasional specimens of either species may exceed 5 feet (1.5 m).

If hibernated, fox snakes can be bred. Egg clutches are large, often exceeding 20 eggs. An incubation temperature of 80 to 86°F (27–30°C) is suggested. The foot-long hatchlings usually feed readily and grow quickly.

air conditioning and winter heating reduce the humidity, these snakes do well. However, for the most part, we do not consider either species of *Bogertophis* beginners' snakes. Additionally, we feel they are poor candidates for breeding programs even by advanced hobbyists when located in humid areas of the country.

The Trans-Pecos Rat Snake

Range: The overall distribution of *B. s. subocularis* is from central New Mexico and western Texas southward to the Mexican states of Durango and Nuevo Leon. This is a beautiful creature that occurs in three distinct morphs besides having a poorly known, quite different central Mexican subspecies.

1. The "normal" phase of *B. s. subocularis* occurs over most of the range of the species. The ground color of this morph is straw to olive-yellow. The neck is marked with a pair of (usually) distinct black dorsolateral stripes that fades and becomes H-shaped blotches on the body. The arms of each H are formed by a darkening of the dorsolateral stripes. The crossbar of each H may be as dark as the arms and considerably paler or lacking entirely. (The latter seems especially apt to occur on captive-bred and hatched specimens.) Poorly defined lateral blotches are often evident.

2. A "blonde" morph occasionally occurs in the lower Pecos River drainage (especially near Terlingua, Texas). The ground color of this phase is much yellower than normal and the dorsolateral striping (even on the neck) is either muted or absent. Rather than H's, the body markings are in the form of light-centered, irregular saddles. Lateral blotches may, or may not, be present.

3. The third morph is less well known. The markings are like those of the normal phase but, rather than being yellow, the ground color is pale

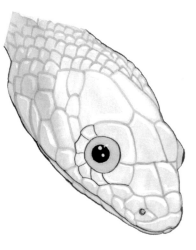

Both the Baja and the Trans-Pecos rat snakes display a unique row of scales under the eye.

to steel-gray. These gray subocs seem restricted in distribution to the Franklin Mountains, a mountain range near El Paso, Texas.

An even prettier and more uniformly gray phase is now being bred by a few breeders. This phase is often referred to as the silver morph. It is quite different in appearance and sells for much higher prices than the normal subocs.

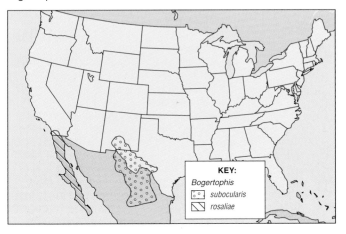

KEY:

Bogertophis

⬡ *subocularis*

⬛ *rosaliae*

Both normal colored (left) and blonde (right) Trans-Pecos rat snakes are now bred in captivity. These are nocturnal snakes with large eyes.

Mexican subspecies: Because the snake is protected in Mexico, no examples of the subspecies, *B. s. amplinotus*, are known in herpetoculture. In this race the neck striping is dark and of uniform width and the dark blotches are variable and seldom in the form of H's. The dark blotches are wider than the light interspaces and the dark lateral spots are very evident; thus the snake appears to be dark with light barring. This is in direct contrast to the nominate form that always appears to be a light snake with dark blotches. *B. s. amplinotus* seems restricted in distribution to the southernmost periphery of the range of the species.

Diet: Although these snakes reach a fairly large size and bulk, captives prefer small prey items. Those adults we have kept accepted baby mice or a few newborn rats, but no larger mice and/or furred baby rats. Although these snakes can constrict, ours simply pinned their live prey with a coil and began swallowing at the head. (Ours were generally given prekilled food items.) Hatchlings prefer small lizards, especially the side-blotched lizard, *Uta stansburiana*, or anoles, *Anolis* sp.

Size: In size, the Trans-Pecos rat snake may reach 5.5 feet (1.665 m).

Reproduction: The Trans-Pecos tends to be a late breeder, with the female going through two (or, rarely, three) post-hibernation sheds before being ready to breed. Breeding can occur as late as June, with the eggs being deposited in August or September. From three to seven eggs are laid. The eggs should be incubated from 82 to 86°F (28–30°C).

Availability: In its normal phase the Trans-Pecos rat snake is both readily available and relatively inexpensive. Blonde phase specimens are in more limited supply and generally cost at least twice as much as the normals. The silver morph is in short supply and is, at present, very expensive. The *B. s. amplinotus* of Durango and Nuevo Leon is unavailable at present.

The Baja California Rat Snake

Range: The known range of the Baja California rat snake is strangely disjunct. We know with certainty that it occurs over much of the Mexican state of Baja California Sur to at least the latitude of the Gulf of California town of Santa Rosalia. North of Santa

Rosalia the snake is known from isolated records in Baja California Norte and in Imperial County, California. These isolated sightings suggest that the actual range of *B. rosaliae* may be much greater than is now known. Rather than being rare, it is the isolation of the range and habitat of this species that assures it will remain uncommon in herpetoculture. Additionally, Mexican wildlife laws prohibit the collecting and exportation of this species to the United States except under specific permitation.

Coloration: This pretty, but blandly colored, snake is almost unicolored when adult and hardly any better patterned when small. Hatchlings are so light in color that they appear translucent. The adult coloration may vary by specimen from olive-tan to reddish-brown. The babies are paler and have thin, poorly defined white (or at least lighter) dorsal crossbands.

Diet: Despite their good size and bulk, captives like small prey items such as baby mice, and will usually accept newborn rats. Our specimens would refuse larger mice and furred baby rats. Although capable of constricting, ours tended instead to immobilize the live prey with a single loop and swallow it. More often than not, the snakes were given prekilled food items. Although a few hatchlings will feed on newly born mice, all quite obviously prefer suitably sized lizards. The favorite lizard type seem to be side-blotched lizards, *Uta stansburiana*, followed by anoles, *Anolis* sp.

Size: The largest Baja rat snake yet measured was 58 inches (147 cm); most are 4 feet (1.2 m) or less in total length.

Reproduction: The Baja California rat snake is another late-breeding snake, with the post-hibernation female shedding two or three times before breeding. Breeding may not

Few specimens of the the Baja rat snake, E. rosaliae, *have been collected. However, a few hobbyists are keeping and breeding this species.*

occur until June. Eggs are deposited in August or September.

Availability: Specialty breeders occasionally offer hatchlings of *B. rosaliae* to the public. The cost of these remains several hundred dollars per snake. Despite this high price, offered specimens are usually snapped up quickly. The facts that there are few breeding size Baja rat snakes in U.S. collections, that they are not the easiest of the rat snakes to breed, and that those that do breed produce small clutches will keep the price of the species high in the foreseeable future.

The Green Rat Snake and Relatives

The author sat one long ago evening in a campground in the Chiricahua Mountains of southeastern Arizona. Rather than sleeping, he sat up for most of the evening. The campsite was visited by skunks, raccoons, and coatis, and late in the evening by a rather special reptile that made staying awake worthwhile.

That reptile was a green rat snake, *Senticolis triaspis intermedia* (then

The several subspecies of Senticolis triaspis *vary from greenish* (intermedia) *in the north to even browner* (triaspis) *than the pictured example. Seen here is a* S. t. mutabilis *from Nicaragua. Photographed at Glades Herp.*

Both were within a very few miles of the first.

The author was even luckier than he first thought, for, apparently, the northernmost specimens of the green rat snake are supposed to be diurnal and crepuscular, rather than nocturnal. One of the other live sightings was crossing a dirt road near Paradise, Arizona during a midnight thunderstorm and the DOR was found late at night between passes on a roadway near Portal, Arizona. The final north-of-the-border specimen was sighted low in a roadside shrub at midafternoon on an overcast day.

The *intermedia* seen in Mexico were active during warm weather nighttime thunderstorms in the Mexican state of Colima; however, there the subspecies is more apt to be brownish than green.

To see green rat snakes in their preferred habitat in the United States, walk along rocky, intermittent streams that run through oak, sycamore, willow, and pine-forested canyons in the Chiricahua (and other nearby) moun-

Elaphe chlorosoma). It was the first that he had seen in the wild, and to this day, he has seen only a few others and most of those have been deep in Mexico. In fact, despite numerous trips to southeastern Arizona, he has seen only two other live (and one DOR— dead on the road) specimens of the green rat snake north of the border.

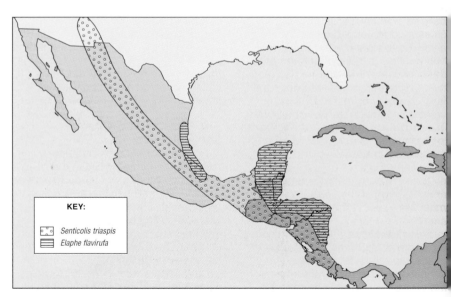

KEY:

Senticolis triaspis
Elaphe flavirufa

tain ranges. Even though we've never yet found a rat snake by doing this, there is so much else to look at that we were not disappointed.

The genus *Senticolis* (sen-tick-ah-lis) is another of the recent spinoffs from *Elaphe*. *Senticolis* contains only the species *triaspis*, which in turn contains a questionable number (probably three) of subspecies. (The subspecies are so variable that it is difficult to tell where one ends and another begins.)

Range: Senticolis is basically a Latin American genus, with the single species being common (but secretive) and widely distributed from extreme southeastern Arizona to eastern Costa Rica.

Description: The head is distinctive in shape, being elongate, somewhat flattened, and rather broad temporally. At the tip, the snout is rather square.

The most northerly green rat snakes truly are green, at least when they are adults. The juveniles are rather prominently marked with black-edged brown dorsal saddles and lateral blotches against a yellowish ground color. The belly (of both juveniles and adults) is usually an unmarked yellow. Most adults in Arizona and extreme northern Mexico have lost traces of pattern with advancing age. The overall color of these northernmost snakes may vary from olive to gray-green, or, rarely, somewhat brighter. As the range progresses southward, there is a tendency for the snakes to become browner.

Second subspecies: In Central America, the green rat snake is a pretty reddish-brown in ground color and is thought to be of the subspecies *mutabilis*. Like the race *intermedia*, as adulthood is reached, the blotched pattern of *mutabilis* becomes obscured and large adults are almost (or entirely) unicolored.

Third subspecies: Unlike the two races already mentioned, *Senticolis tri-* *aspis triaspis* from the Yucatan Peninsula, Belize, and adjacent Guatemala, retains what is commonly called "the juvenile pattern" throughout its life. This, the nominate subspecies, *S. t. triaspis*, is found both in variable thorn scrub forest and on more open agricultural lands. It has been found crossing busy Mexican Route 180 at night near the Mayan ruins of Chichen Itza. The specimens seen, whether juvenile or adult, had dark-edged brown dorsal and lateral blotches, prominent against a ground color of reddish-brown. The ground color is often noticeably lighter (almost white) where it abuts against the dark blotch edges.

Captive care: Whether you call it the green rat snake, the Yucatan rat snake, or some other contrived common name, most hobbyists consider *Senticolis triaspis* a difficult captive. This seems especially so of specimens from the northern portion of the range. Like many subtropical snakes (especially those that feed opportunistically on lizards, frogs, and endothermic prey), wild-collected *S. triaspis* usually harbor a great load of endoparasites. It is imperative that these be purged for any degree of success, but when the parasite and bacterial load has been lessened, *S. triaspis* can prove problematic. Although in habitat it is often considered a streamside species, captives fare poorly if subjected to high relative humidity. Northernmost specimens seem particularly prone to respiratory ailments and digestion problems. The northernmost specimens also seem particularly distressed by both warm and cold temperature extremes. They prefer, and fare best, when temperatures are maintained in the mid-70s°F (21–24°C). Specimens from the southern regions seem less sensitive.

Diet: This is one of the rat snake species that prefers small-sized meals.

Pinky mice will usually be eaten and digested; mice of larger sizes may be refused, or, if eaten, later regurgitated. Males, which seem to be the smaller sex, are particularly reluctant to accept sizable rodents. Wild-caught individuals show a definite preference for wild, rather than domestic, mouse species. Hatchlings of all subspecies seem to prefer lizards over rodents.

Needs in captivity: Despite all of these problems, green rat snakes and their more southerly relatives are eagerly sought by advanced breeders. Prices are high for specimens, whether acclimated or freshly collected from the wild. These finicky snakes demand fairly elaborate facilities with temperature and humidity control. Adequate cover will help these nervous snakes feel at home. Captives we have maintained climbed actively through branches (although in nature, this species seems far less arboreal than is often suggested), as often after darkness had fallen as before.

Breeding: A few specialist breeder-hobbyists have succeeded keeping and breeding green rat snakes. Most of these people live in areas very

The females of many rat snakes may remain with their eggs for several days. This is a female Elaphe flavirufa *ssp. with her small clutch of large eggs.*

close to the natural habitat of the snakes, i.e., Arizona, New Mexico, and southern California. A period of winter dormancy seems as mandatory for successful long-term husbandry as for reproductive cycling. Brumation is a critical period for these snakes, and normal techniques can result in temporary or semipermanent neurological distress. It has been found by one hobbyist that when a "hot spot" is retained near the hibernaculum, cooled *Senticolis* will often preferentially keep their heads and anterior bodies warmed while positioning their posterior body in the cooled hibernaculum. Snakes cooled with this unique regimen seem to display no neurological problems following "hibernation." However, other individuals who work with green rat snakes merely cool them the same as they do other montane species and report no unusual problems when the snakes are warmed the next spring.

A 40-inch-long (101.6 cm) gravid female *S. t. mutabilis* that we received laid four large eggs. The slightly less than foot-long hatchlings emerged after an incubation period of nearly two months at room temperature (in Florida this varied from 79 to 85°F [26–29°C]). Female *S. triaspis* seem to attain a greater size than the males. Females of more than 5 feet (1.5 m) have been found; males seem seldom to exceed 4.25 feet (1.28 m) in total length.

A Latin American Corn Snake Lookalike

The *Elaphe flavirufa* is another of the many rat snake species with no accepted common name. The few times we have seen a common name used, it has been Mexican corn snake. Since the species ranges well south of Mexico, the name is not entirely accurate. Although uncommonly imported, *E. flavirufa* is a beautiful and, once purged of endoparasites, hardy species. The ground color is gray and the black-edged dorsal and lateral markings vary from strawberry to maroon in coloration. As noted in the chart, the dorsal markings may be discrete blotches or may be connected for all or part of the length of the snake. This species darkens noticeably with age and some very old adults are much less attractive than younger specimens.

There may be up to five (poorly differentiated) subspecies. They are so poorly differentiated that it is more time efficient to prepare a rough key than to attempt written descriptions. Listed are the criteria currently used in the subspecific differentiations. Please note that in virtually all cases there is a chance of overlap.

In reality, these snakes currently reach the pet market in such small numbers that which subspecies becomes available is of little consequence. Hobbyists, who are interested in pairing their animals, will purchase whichever it happens to be. If this happens to actually be a pair of one given

Although not a commonly seen captive, E. flavirufa ssp. *is a pretty and hardy Tropical American rat snake.*

subspecies, so much the better, but if a male of one subspecies and a female of another have been imported, they are usually sold and purchased as a pair. Subspecies can interbreed, and since there is neither chance nor necessity for releasing the snakes back to the wild, intergradation would mean little to most hobbyists.

Subspecies	dorsal blotches mostly connected (zigzag)	dorsal blotches discrete	lateral blotches well defined	lateral blotches absent	preocular divided X undivided Y
flavirufa	X		X		Y
pardalina	X		X		X; 31 scale rows
polysticha	X		X		X; more than 32 scale rows
phaescens		X	X		
matudai		X		X	

The ranges of the various subspecies are:

flavirufa: the east coast of Mexico, from the state of Tamaulipas southward to Campeche

pardalina: mainland Guatemala, Honduras, and Nicaragua

polysticha: Caribbean Islands of Honduras

phaescens: Mexico's Yucatan Peninsula

matudai: poorly known; southeastern Mexico

Eyes: As noticeable, perhaps, as the pretty colors and intricate patterns of *E. flavirufa* are its eyes. The eyes are proportionately large and have stark white irises, reflecting the nocturnal tendencies of this rat snake.

Size: These snakes reputedly attain more than 5 feet (1.5 m) in length, but 26 to 40 inches (66–101.6 cm) is more common.

Reproduction: Although the various *E. flavirufa* come from areas that are subtropical in climate, some come from the cool, rather dry areas of this very indefinite climatic designation, and others from warm and quite humid areas. Since we have not personally bred this species, we can offer only suggestions for its herpetoculture. We would subject them to a period of winter cooling (but not true hibernation) for a period of 60 to 90 days.

Our largest specimen, a 40-inch (101.6 cm) female, was gravid when received. She eventually deposited five eggs that were incubated at room temperature (79–85°F [26–29°C]). The incubation period (although not specifically recorded) was in the vicinity of 60 days. The hatchlings had a paler ground color than the female.

Diet: *E. flavirufa* seems to prefer meals both small in amount and in size. At least in captivity, they are not an overly active snake. If purged of all endoparasites and not otherwise unduly stressed, one or two "jumper" mice (young, furred, active mice), once weekly, will suffice to maintain even a moderately sized specimen in good health.

Behavior: A single specimen that the author found in the field was crossing a roadway in southern Tamaulipas on a rather cool, very rainy July night. When picked up, it made no attempt to bite. However, specimens seen at dealers have flattened their heads and struck repeatedly at the approach of a hand, being, in effect, a very typical rat snake in attitude.

Species Accounts: Old World Rat Snakes

European and Eurasian Rat Snakes

Although routinely kept in Europe, European rat snakes are not common in America. Those that are imported by dealers are usually hatchlings and are quite expensive. Many also have a reputation among American hobbyists for being delicate, which perhaps can be attributed to the American mindset for keeping reptiles in the simplest possible way. On the other hand, European hobbyists have a tendency construct elaborate terrarium environments.

Of course, another factor may figure in—shipping. At best, shipping is stressful for herptiles. Most Europeans acquire their European rat snakes by hand, carrying them from origin to terrarium. In America, specimens must be shipped, which takes from two to four days of temperature variations, inspections, air pressure variations, and bouncing about. If the rat snake is then dropped into an unadorned plastic shoebox, it's small wonder that these snakes are considered delicate. Regarding expense, European hobbyists covet their rat snakes and few breed as readily as the American corn and yellow rats. Most (if not all) European countries also now largely prohibit collecting reptiles and amphibians from the wild. Since virtually all specimens that are available are captive-bred and hatched, eager and sophisticated European hobbyists provide a ready market. Those who hope to work with the European species must be willing to pay for them.

Of the four species of *Elaphe* that occur in Europe, only the ladder rat snake, *Elaphe scalaris*, is restricted to that continent. The other three are found well into western Asia; therefore, they are actually of Eurasian distribution. Only one species, the leopard rat snake, *E. situla*, is brightly colored as an adult.

A final note before moving on: All European rat snakes seem to need lengthy periods (80 +/- days) of full hibernation (at 48–54°F [9–12°C]) to cycle reproductively. Sadly, many European rat snakes seem particularly prone to respiratory problems during hibernation. Use care and inspect your animals often, but do not expect to breed them without this period of complete dormancy.

At a temperature of 79–82°F (26–28°C), the incubation duration for the eggs of all European rat snakes ranges from about 58 to 75 days. Although some hobbyists prefer the lower temperature, we have had the best success with 81–82°F (27–28°C).

The Ladder Rat Snake (*Elaphe scalaris*)

A good alternate name for the young adults of this moderately sized rat snake would be "two-lined rat snake." The dark transverse bars of the busily patterned young become obscured with increasing age, leaving only a pair of dorsolateral lines. A dark postorbital blotch angles downward to or beneath the rear of the jaw in younger specimens, while only traces

Because of its "H-shaped" dorsal markings, E. scalaris *is commonly referred to as the "ladder rat snake."*

but may be suffused with dark pigment. The ground color of juvenile specimens is brighter. The ladder of the juveniles and adult lines are darker brown than the ground color. This is an interesting, but not brightly colored, snake.

Size: Although adults of the ladder snake occasionally attain a length of more than 5 feet (1.5 m), most individuals range from 4 to 4.5 feet (1.2–1.37 m) in length.

Range: The range of *E. scalaris* is restricted to the Iberian Peninsula, southern coastal areas of adjacent France, and some outlying islands. It prefers dry, rather open habitats, and is typically encountered in terrestrial situations in agricultural areas, open, rocky woodlands, hedgerows, and near rock walls, all favored basking sites.

Habits: Wild specimens bite readily. They are reputedly largely diurnal in the wild. The very few specimens that we have kept have seemed most active in the late afternoon and at dusk, and more readily accepted food then.

Diet: Although the adults strongly prefer endothermic prey of moderate size (mice, small rats, birds, etc.), the diet of the juveniles can also include lizards, frogs, insects, and what baby endotherms they happen across.

Captive breeding: This species has been bred in Europe and America. Typically, clutches number between four and nine rather large eggs (see the introductory section of this chapter for hibernation and breeding specifics).

are retained by adults. The markings of some old adults can be almost totally obscured.

Scalaris is of variable disposition also. Wild-collected adults can be savage, but many captive-bred animals are rather tractible.

Color: The ground color of adults may vary between brown, brownish-olive to yellow-olive dorsally and laterally. The venter is somewhat brighter, often yellowish or off-white in color,

The Four-Lined Rat Snake (*Elaphe quatuorlineata* ssp.)

Pattern and subspecies: The young of all races of this, the largest European rat snake, are prominently blotched middorsally and laterally, a pattern retained by the adults of one of the subspecies, *E. q. sauromates.* Other subspecies (*E. q. praematura* and *E. q. muenteri*) tend to retain the

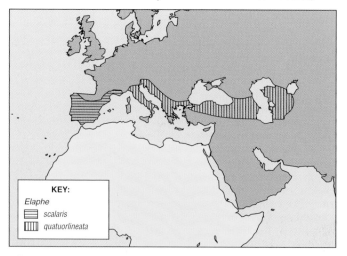

KEY:
Elaphe
▤ *scalaris*
▥ *quatuorlineata*

juvenile pattern, but develop stripes as well. Of the four races, the nominate, *E. q. quatuorlineata*, is the most apt to lose all vestiges of the juvenile pattern and to develop well-defined lines, best described by the accepted common name. All subspecies have a short, downwardly inclined bar from the rear of the eye to the angle of the jaw.

In both ontogeny and variability by subspecies, this European/Asiatic rat snake is quite similar to the American *E. obsoleta* complex.

Although often not as prone to bite as other European species of rat snake, we would not go so far as to dub this snake the "gentle giant," as some keepers have.

Range: The prominently blotched *E. q. sauromates* occupies an extensive range. It may be encountered from northeastern Greece and southeastern Bulgaria through the Danube region to the Caucasus, Asia Minor, and Iran. A smaller subspecies, *sauromates* seldom exceeds 4.5 feet (1.37 m) in total length. Both of the striped *and* spotted races, *E. q. praematura* and *E. q. muenteri*, are of Aegean distribution. *E. q. praematura* occurs on the island of Jos (Cyclades) and *E. q. muenteri* on other Aegean Islands. Both are of rather small adult size (3.5–4.5 feet [1.06–1.37 m]).

The large *E. q. quatuorlineata* is the most westerly ranging of the four races. It occurs from southern Italy to Greece and the southern Balkans. Although an adult reaches 8 feet (2.4 m), 4.5 to 6 feet (1.06–1.8 m) is more typical.

Coloration: *E. q. quatuorlineata* undergoes great color and pattern changes as it matures from juvenile to adult. The hatchlings and juveniles are prominently spotted with dark dorsal and lateral blotches on a pale gray or tan background. The top of the head is spotted and a large nape blotch that is divided posteriorly (or at least contains

The blotches now so prominent on this baby European four-lined rat snake (E. q. quatuorlineata) *will fade with age.*

a light center) is evident. With growth, the spots, including those on the surface of the head and the nape, obscure and the four dark lines for which the species has been named become increasingly prominent. The dark postorbital bar is usually retained. The ground color darkens to deep tan, brownish olive, or light brown. The ground color is darkest vertebrally, hence palest laterally. The top of the head is brown and the lips are light.

Breeding: Clutch size of this species varies. A clutch from a small female *E. q. sauromates* that bred during her third summer numbered only three eggs. Conversely, a clutch from a big, healthy, older female *E. q. quatuorlineata* numbered 18 eggs (see the introductory section in this chapter for information on hibernation and breeding).

Diet: *E. quatuorlineata* is one of the hardier and more voracious of the European rat snakes. Although hatchlings may show a preference for lizards, most will readily accept pinky mice. Larger-sized snakes will accept correspondingly larger mice or small rats.

(The snake known previously as *E. q. rechingeri* is mentioned in some more detail in the following account of *E. longissima*.)

The Aesculapian Rat Snake (*Elaphe longissima*)

The often gentle *E. longissima* was considered sacred by the ancient Greeks and has since been associated with Aesculapias, the Greek god of medicine. A caricature of this species is depicted on the medical caduceus.

Color: Of the three noncolorful European rat snake species, this species is the most bland. Adults are olive-tan to olive-green and may bear the vaguest vestiges of dorsolateral striping and/or light flecking. A dark postocular bar is very visible on juvenile specimens and, although faded, may be retained into adulthood. Except for their smooth scales, hatchlings and juveniles of the Aesculapian rat snake look remarkably like the young of *Natrix natrix*, the grass snake—complete to the alternating dorsal and lateral checkers and the yellow to off-white temporal blotches. There are three poorly defined subspecies.

The snake on the medical caduceus is the Aesculapian rat snake.

Range: Only *E. l. longissima* has been available to American hobbyists. The nominate form ranges from the eastern Iberian Peninsula eastward through southern Europe, to extreme northwestern Iran.

The rat snake from the island of Amorgos has been variously considered a race of the Aesculapian rat snake, *E. longissima*, a variant of *E. quatuorlineata*, or a full species (*E. rechingeri*). What this snake is called at any given moment depends on the interpretation by the researcher. Variably colored, the adults can have poorly defined stripes or be virtually unicolored, and the younger specimens are considerably paler than those of other races. *E. l. persica*, a dark-bellied race, occurs in northern Iran, and *E. l. romana*, a variably striped form, is from southern Italy and Sicily.

Habitat: Like other European rat snakes, *E. longissima* is a primarily terrestrial snake associated with dry, sandy, sunny habitats that provide cover in the form of vines or other open vegetation. Old rock walls, hedgerows, ruins, and dry, open woodlands are also prime habitat.

Diet: Our specimens preferred meals of several small, rather than one or two large, mice. Hatchlings and juveniles will eagerly accept lizards. Most will, however, quickly convert to meals of pinky mice.

Hibernation: *E. longissima* needs a lengthy (80 +/– days) hibernation (at 48–54°F [9–12°C]). Watch for any signs of respiratory problems during this period.

Incubation: When incubated at 79–82°F (26–28°C), eggs will hatch in 58 to 75 days. We have had better success with the high end of the spectrum, from 81–82°F (27–28°C).

The Leopard Snake (*Elaphe situla*)

We come now to the crown jewel of European rat snakes. As a matter

Although not brightly colored, the Aesculapian rat snake is gentle and hardy.

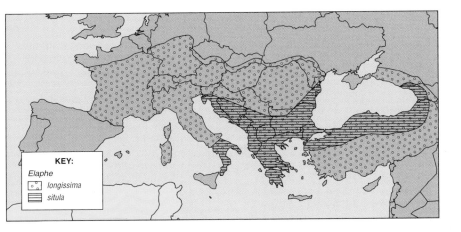

KEY:
Elaphe
[o o] *longissima*
[≡] *situla*

of fact, the leopard rat snake—a corn snake lookalike—is one of the most beautiful members of the entire genus, including the corn snake. Baby specimens that are not used to handling may bite repeatedly, but with gentle handling, leopard snakes soon tame.

Size: The leopard rat snake is the smallest of the European rat snakes. An average size for adults is between 26 and 30 inches (66–75.6 cm). An occasional exceptional specimen may near 40 inches (101.6 cm) in length.

Habitat: Like other European rat snakes, *E. situla* is associated with hot, dry, often sandy, rocky, or sparsely wooded habitats. Within these habitats, the leopard rat snake finds coolness and seclusion in fencerows, ruins, and old stone walls.

Diet: Like many of the small and slender rat snakes of the world, *E. situla* prefers small meals of nestling rodents and ground-dwelling birds. Hatchlings and juveniles often eagerly accept lizards and tree frogs. The several specimens we have had have borne rather heavy loads of endoparasites when received and were initially reluctant to feed. The snakes were individually housed in 20-gallon (75.7 L) terraria that had substrates of fallen leaves atop an inch or two of sandy soil. Those that were reluctant to feed on domestic mice were avid feeders upon small white-footed mice.

Temperature: Leopard rat snakes do not tolerate excessive warmth well. The temperature at which we keep our specimens varies, but is usually between 82 and 85°F (28–29°C) by day in the warmed part of the terrarium and several degrees cooler in the rest of the terrarium. Night temperatures are allowed to fall by several degrees.

The leopard rat snake is one of the most beautiful species of the entire genus.

73

Hibernation: We had been cautioned that preparing a suitable hibernaculum for these snakes would be difficult, but we did not find this to be so. We merely hibernated them in less humid conditions than the other species, and roused them for a lengthy drink at no greater than fortnightly intervals. Under these conditions the snakes tolerated hibernation well.

Reproduction: The earliest we have been able to induce leopard rat snakes to breed was following their second hibernation. The snakes were about 20 months of age and somewhat over 24 inches (60.9 cm) in length. Eggs laid that first season were inviable, but breedings following subsequent hibernations have produced small clutches (two to five) of "good" eggs.

The hatchlings measure just under a foot (.30 m) in length and feed after their postnatal shed. Some eat newly born domestic mice, but most prefer the pinkies of wild mouse and vole species.

Coloration: The purported resemblance between the leopard rat snake and the corn snake is based on blotch color. The blotch arrangement is actually quite different. The "saddles" of the leopard rat snake are actually two rows of dark-edged strawberry dorsolateral spots that may, or may not, be connected vertebrally by dorsal extensions. All, some, or no blotches may be connected dorsally. In the latter case, the dorsolateral markings may be in the form of discrete spots or connected laterally in broken or continuous black-edged, red stripes. Thus, any series of "normal" leopard rat snakes may contain snakes of very variable appearance. The ground color of the leopard rat snake may be gray, olive-gray, tan, or pale olive-green. The head pattern is rather complex. A dark, posteriorly curving bar extends across the top of the head immediately anterior to the eyes. The internasals are usually tipped anteriorly with some black. A diagonal black temporal stripe is present on both sides and a black, or black-edged red marking extends anteriorly from the partially divided nape blotch on to the frontal plate. The venter is predominantly black. Leopard rat snakes are far more slender proportionately than corn snakes.

Availability: Because of their great beauty and comparative rarity, leopard rat snakes are coveted by collectors. Expensive even in Europe, the few that reach the United States may be almost prohibitively so. In spite of this, they are of immense interest and well worth the somewhat specialized care that they require to thrive.

Some Asian Favorites

Because of the initial (and sometimes, continued) belligerence and delicacy of most specimens, Asian rat snakes were long overlooked and underappreciated by herpetoculturists. Now that the Asian representatives of this genus are rarely imported, both European and American hobbyists are initiating breeding programs. Efforts have been successful with some species (*E. taeniura*, etc.), but largely unsuccessful with others (*E. mollendorffi*).

An almost invariable heavy load of internal parasites did much to contribute to the delicacy of those early imported Asian *Elaphe*. Fortunately, parasite treatments have improved exponentially in the last decade. Additionally, our knowledge of the natural history of many species has increased, resulting in better husbandry techniques. Perhaps our previous dislike of being bitten, or its importance to us when choosing an otherwise pretty specimen, has been modified.

There is absolutely no doubt about the feistiness of many Asian rat snake species. The new captives of many types are forever ready to bite. Others, such as the very popular Russian rat snake, *E. schrencki*, are much more placid. These latter are every bit as easy to handle and manage as the North American yellow rat and corn snakes.

Although most of the Asian rat snakes are perfectly capable of constriction, many immobilize their prey by grasping it in their mouth, then throwing a single loop of their body over it. *E. radiata*, *E. taeniura ridleyi* and many of the Asian rat snake relatives (genera *Gonyosoma* and *Spalerosophis*) indulge in this method of prey immobilization.

With advancing age, the saddles of this Amur rat snake will become black. Adult specimens are rather like eastern kingsnakes in color.

The Amur (Russian) Rat Snake, *Elaphe schrencki*

Appearance: An initial glance at the nominate race of *E. schrencki* reminds most viewers of the eastern kingsnake. Adult *E. s. schrencki* are black snakes that are patterned with numerous pale crossbands. The labials are light, often a rather bright yellow with black scale-seams. This brilliance carries over onto the chin and may be present subcaudally as well. The tail is often patterned beneath but may be immaculate (or largely so). The venter is also variable, being light in color and either heavily, sparsely, or virtually unpatterned. Hatchlings and juveniles are prominently marked with dark-edged dorsal saddles of some shade of brown, and tan to gray crossbars. A dark bar begins just posterior to the nostril, extends through the eye, and angles downward to the angle of the jaw.

Captive care: These gentle and powerful constrictors are hardy and easily kept, feeding on suitably sized rodents. Most adults will tackle prey up to the size of medium rats. Both races of this snake frequently exceed 4 feet (1.2 m) in length and may reach 5 feet (1.5 m). One of our particularly large male *E. s. schrencki* measured 73 inches (185 cm)!

Since they come from an area typified by harsh, cool weather, captive Amur rat snakes do not require a lot of auxiliary heat. A cage temperature of 72–76°F (22–24°C)—we do provide an illuminated basking spot of 82–85°F (27.7–29°C)—is satisfactory.

Hibernation: As would be expected of a northern clime snake, hibernation is a necessary part of reproductive cycling. Although a hibernation of up to five months has been suggested, our Amur rat snakes bred well (and regularly) with a standardized 90-day hibernation period. These snakes, cooled to between 47 and 52°F (8.3–11°C), were roused for a drink at two to three week intervals. Clutches numbered from 7 to 16 eggs, occasionally 30.

Two races: The nominate form of *E. schrencki* is the more northerly of the two races. *E. s. schrencki* is found in Siberia, Manchuria, and northeastern Korea. It is replaced in western Korea to northeastern China by the lighter *E. s. anomala*. This latter snake, often referred to as the Korean rat snake, has a ground color of tan, olive-tan, or olive-gray, which brighten posteriorly. The blotches are only vaguely darker and are edged on both leading and trailing margins with buff. The blotches are usually better defined (and darker) from a point two-thirds of the way back to the tailtip. Lip, chin, ventrals, and subcaudals are often a rich, unpatterned yellow. Hatchlings and juveniles are duller than those of *E. s. schrencki*.

Moellendorff's (or Copper-headed) Rat Snake (*Elaphe moellendorffi*)

In contrast to the hardiness of the preceding species, the equally large (6 feet [1.8 m] plus) *E. moellendorffi* is delicate. As with many wild-collected rat snakes, the heavy parasite load borne by most individuals is a significant problem. The mortality of other specimens has been attributed to an irreversible buildup of caseous (cheesy) material in the lung. However, rarely, and with proper purging, a very occasional specimen of this pretty rat snake of somewhat divergent appear-ance has thrived as a captive. Moellendorff's rat snakes can vary in temperament. Some individuals are persistently savage but others will allow gentle handling.

Captive care: *E. moellendorffi* is a powerful and supple constrictor, preferring small prey items. Few specimens will accept domestic mice. Most of the few that do feed prefer rat pups, chicks, or better yet, various wild mice and voles.

Temperature: Moellendorff's rat snakes seem to prefer cool weather and cool habitats, a preference that must be considered in captivity. These snakes are forest-dwellers in southern China and adjacent northern Vietnam. Captives seem to do best when terrarium temperatures are maintained in the low to mid-70s°F (25°C). As with other rat snakes, we provide *E. moel-*

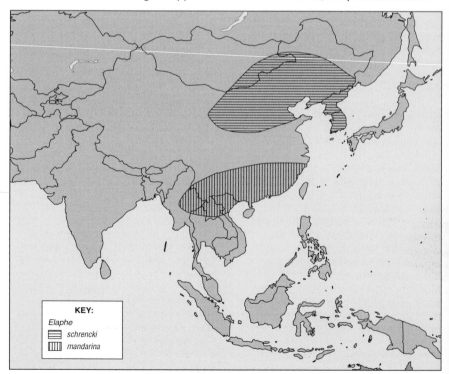

KEY:
Elaphe
schrencki
mandarina

lendorffi with an illuminated basking spot that is a few degrees warmer than the ambient.

Coloration: Although some specimens are duller than others, for the most part, *E. moellendorffi* is an attractive snake. Head coloration may vary from dull copper to a rather bright orange-red. The head is broad temporally, the snout somewhat squared and elongate, and the overall conformation looks very much like that of the New World *Senticolis triaspis* (see page 63). The tail is red with broad, dark-edged maroon rings. The body's ground color is an attractive olive-gray, gray, to silver gray (interstitial skin is lighter than the scales). The brown to reddish-brown dorsal saddles and lateral blotches are usually dark-edged. The dorsal saddles may have lighter centers, but usually do not. Light interstitial skin may be visible both in the ground area and blotches if the snakes are distended with food and/or are tightly coiled. Aberrant colors morphs such as hypomelanism are known, but we have not yet seen them offered in the American pet trade.

Availability: At one time considered a rarity in both the American and European pet markets, *E. moellendorffi* is now imported in fair, but varying, numbers. The price has dropped from three figures (1970s), to usually less than a hundred dollars today. Because of this snake's high (close to 99 percent) and rapid mortality rate, most dealers that now offer Moellendorff's rat snakes have their veterinarian check and purge each specimen for endoparasites; however, even this does not assure success with Moellendorff's rat snakes. With this species, perhaps more than any other rat snake, veterinary assessment and intervention is a necessity rather than an option.

Chris Newman, an English herpetoculturist, is currently delving into the

Herpetoculturists have a dismal record with the beautiful Moellendorff's rat snake. Our repeated failures prompt us to suggest that this species should not be collected from the wild for the pet trade.

natural history of Moellendorff's rat snake in China. Newman hopes, through information given him by new and knowledgeable contacts, to be able to develop a truly successful breeding program with this species.

Breeding: Despite being rather readily available in the pet trade, *E. moellendorffi* is seldom bred in captivity. Most of the very *few* captive-hatched specimens that have become available have resulted from eggs deposited by females that were gravid when imported. Strangely, however, no matter what time of year the snakes are imported, gravid females are seldom seen. This is in sharp contrast with virtually all other species of rat snakes. Eggs of this species are fairly large but the clutch size is small (4 to 11 eggs). Captive longevity of over 21 years has been reported by one zoo.

The Mandarin Rat Snake (*Elaphe mandarina*)

This gentle snake is another of the rather atypical-appearing Asian rat snakes. The head of *E. mandarina* is

77

Many specimens of the Mandarin rat snake have a more clean-cut pattern than this attractive example. This is another difficult to keep species. Photographed at Glades Herp.

narrow and not well differentiated from the neck, while the snout is short and rounded.

Coloration: *E. mandarina* is one of the least variable of the Asian rat snakes. The dorsal saddles are dia-mond-shaped with bright yellow centers. The black of the saddles may extend downward to the ventral plates and, in addition, there may be irregular black lateral markings. The head has black rostral markings, a black supra-orbital bar connects the eyes, and a pair of black subocular triangles are present. An anteriorly directed black chevron is present on the rear of the head, bordered posteriorly by a yellow chevron. The yellow venter may be extensively spotted or crossbanded with black. The ground color may be olive-fawn, pale gray, or olive-gray. Some (apparently few) specimens have the dorsal blotches fragmented and broken; however, with these, it is the pattern, not the coloration that is changed.

Size: Although *E. mandarina* of slightly more than 5 feet (1.5 m) in total length are known, most are between 30 and 40 inches (76–101.6 cm) long.

Habits: *E. mandarina* is a montane species found in northern Burma,

northern Vietnam, and southern and eastern China. The first recorded specimens were found at altitudes above 2,000 feet (608 m) on forested slopes and plateaus. Additionally, *E. mandarina* is preferentially crepuscular and nocturnal. Temperatures, espe-cially night temperatures, are relatively cool and the humidity fairly high in such habitats.

Captive care: Captive specimens respond best to temperatures in the high 60s to mid-70s°F (20.25°C). Our captives have shown a reluctance to bask in brilliantly illuminated "hot spots" but would thermoregulate over a heat tape. The warmest spot in their terrarium approached 84°F (28.8°C).

Early specimens: Mandarin rat snakes were only rarely imported in the 1970s. Many of those early speci-mens were already weak when imported and refused to feed. Although others ate, they as quickly regurgitated and soon succumbed. Postmortems revealed heavy parasite loads. In the 1980s, however, additional specimens became available, many in relatively good condition. The imported snakes were wormed and began eating the smallest of meals. Some preferred newly born rats over mice, while oth-ers would eagerly accept newly hatched button quail. Many would accept wild mice but refuse all other foods. Small meals are much less likely to be regurgitated.

Behavior: Even the best accli-mated of Mandarin rat snakes are secretive. Those that we have kept burrowed avidly in cypress bark mulch or dry, unmilled, sphagnum moss. Captives seem to stress easily, and newly fed specimens will often regurgi-tate if handled. Mandarin rat snakes are not easily cycled to reproductive readiness nor do they always feed when we think they should. We con-sider them a species for advanced hobbyists. Imported specimens are usually very heavily parasitized. It is imperative that endoparasites be eradicated as soon as possible.

Breeding: The very few captive breedings that have occurred have followed a normal (90 +/- day) period of hibernation. Hatchlings are between 11 and 13 inches (27.9–33 cm) in length.

The Striped-Tailed Rat Snakes (*Elaphe taeniura*)

Several races of this attractive species were earlier called "beauty snakes," with a prefix such as Taiwan, Chinese, or Yunnan, which supposedly designated their point of origin. In reality, the common names were often as muddled then as they are now. Once the actual origin of this snake (or actually of many snakes) becomes confused or obscured (as it often does during pet trade shipping), true identification becomes nearly impossible.

Subspecies ID: For many years, the only race of *E. taeniura* seen in the American pet trade was called *E. t. friesei.* Because of its distribution, this pretty but feisty snake was given the common name of Taiwan beauty snake. This race seems to differ only in the *average* number of ventral scales (see Table, page 80) from the nominate form, *E. t. taeniura,* of the Chinese mainland, Burma and Thailand.

Appearance: The many races of *E. taeniura* vary tremendously in external appearance. Some (*taeniura* and *friesei*) are proportionately heavy-bodied, strongly blotched anteriorly, striped posteriorly, and have a ground color of olive-buff to olive-yellow-green. The reddish *E. t. schmackeri* tends to be a little more attenuate, weakly blotched anteriorly, and more strongly so posteriorly. The posterior, light, middorsal stripe, if present, is frequently interrupted, or at least strongly encroached upon, by the posterior blotches. Some subspecies (*grabowskyi* and *ridleyi*) are whipsnake

Hybridization and intergradation are often induced in captive breedings. Bruce Morgan produced these Yunnan x Taiwan stripe-tailed rat snakes.

thin, of light coloration, lack anterior blotches, and are cleanly striped for the posterior three-fifths of their length. Both of these latter snakes are frequently found in or near caves and feed upon bats. *E. t. vaillanti* tends to be intermediate in appearance between the heavy, blotched forms and the attenuate racer-like subspecies. Often referred to as the Yunnan striped-tailed rat snake and designated scientifically (and erroneously) as *E. t. yunnanensis*

The Taiwan stripe-tailed rat snake is now frequently bred in captivity.

Subspecies of E. taeniura	Number of ventrals	Range
friesei	240–260	Taiwan
grabowskyi	275–290	Borneo to Malaysia
ridleyi	more than 280	Thailand to Sumatra
schmackeri	250–260	Ryukyu Islands
taeniura	230–250	Thailand, Burma, southeastern China
vaillanti (=yunnanensis)	220–260	Northern Vietnam and adjacent China, including Yunnan Province

Note that the number of ventral scales of some of the races of this variable species differ widely from other races. Many of these observations and counts, now decades old, were made from a very limited number of specimens. All data is badly in need of updating. Some races of this snake may be reevaluated.

by dealers, *E. t. vaillanti* tends to have less well-defined anterior body blotches than other blotched forms.

Breeding: Only the Taiwan striped-tailed rat snake and the Yunnan striped-tailed rat snake have been bred. Two methods, one with hibernation, the other with cooling, are used to induce reproductive cycling with about equal success. The first involves the use of a 90-day period of virtually complete brumation (hibernation). The snakes are roused every two weeks or so and allowed to drink. Except for their fortnightly drink, the specimens are maintained in complete darkness while hibernating.

Evidently not all striped-tailed rat snakes actually need a period of full hibernation to cycle reproductively. A very successful breeder in southern Florida merely "cools" his specimens during the months of winter by opening the windows in his breeding facility. A natural photoperiod is provided. The falling night temperatures and shortened hours of illumination seem to adequately cycle and stimulate his breeders and the snakes are always alert enough to drink when thirsty.

(Fully hibernated snakes need no food; cooled snakes require food, but more infrequently, and, they eat smaller-sized prey.)

We attempted for many years to breed *E. t. ridleyi*. The year after we parted with the snakes, their new owner, using seemingly identical methods, did succeed in breeding them but his success was not again duplicated, proving only that when it comes to breeding, the snakes themselves ultimately make the decision.

Eggs: Depending on their size, age, and condition, females deposit 14 or fewer eggs. Incubation duration is somewhat more than 60 days at temperatures between 82 and 86°F (28–30°C). The robust hatchlings, which look like smaller and duller adults, often near 15 inches (38 cm) in length at the time of emergence.

Size: Commonly attaining a length of more than 6 feet (1.8 m), *E. t. ridleyi* is so slender that even the longest individuals appear smaller than their actual size. The published record size for *E. t. friesei* is 7 feet 9 inches (2.36 m) but specimens of more than 5.5 feet (1.67 m) are fairly uncommon.

Range: The habitats of the races of *E. taeniura* vary considerably, with elevations ranging from sea level to near 11,000 feet (3,344 m). The snake is found southward from northern China throughout southeast Asia to Sumatra.

Captive care: The various races of *E. taeniura* readily accept adult mice and subadult rats. Imported specimens are often heavily parasitized. Endoparasites must be identified and eradicated for successful hibernation or breeding. Specimens of *E. taeniura* that we have kept have seemed most content when kept cool. Terrarium temperature is usually kept between 70 and 76°F (21–24°C). An illuminated basking area with a temperature of about 86°F (30°C) is provided. The snakes only sometimes avail themselves of the warmth—especially if traffic is heavy near their cage.

We consider all of the various subspecies rather easily kept but moderately difficult-to-difficult serpents to breed. Err toward coolness rather than heat.

The Radiated (or Copperhead) Rat Snake (*Elaphe radiata*)

Behavior: There could hardly be a more defensive colubrine species than wild-caught adults of this interesting and pretty Asian rat snake. When even vaguely threatened, the radiated (so-called for the three dark lines that radiate outward from the eye) pulls its neck back, inflates its throat, and vigorously defends itself. Since adults can exceed a 6 foot (1.8 m) length by several inches, the striking range is fairly extensive.

If possible, radiated rat snakes would prefer to avoid confrontation by fleeing. They are a fast-moving species, the flight actions more like that of a racer than of a typical rat snake.

Breeding: It is only recently that radiated rat snakes have been captive-

Radiated rat snakes collected from the wild can be nervous and aggressive. This specimen has rubbed his nose in the shipping bag. Photographed at Gulf Coast Reptiles.

bred in America. Until these successes, all specimens were wild-collected imports. Although the clutches of *E. radiata* are small (usually three to nine eggs, rarely to a dozen), females are known to have several clutches in the course of a single season. The hatchlings are small, often less than 10 inches (25 cm) in overall length.

Diet: Some wild-collected *E. radiata* can be problematic feeders. Housing them in sizable, quiet terraria may help overcome their reluctance to eat. Also, vary the type of food animals offered—a small rat, a large mouse, a baby chick or quail. Babies will usually readily accept pinky mice.

Coloration: Unlike many of its Asian congenerics, the radiated rat snake is striped anteriorly rather than posteriorly. The four stripes—two heavy dorsolateral stripes and two more poorly defined lateral stripes—are of variable length and best defined on the anterior trunk. Striping may fade by midbody or continue almost to the tail. The ground color of *E. radiata* is also variable, from buff, tan, light brown, or coppery-russet, to yellowish or greenish. The three dark stripes

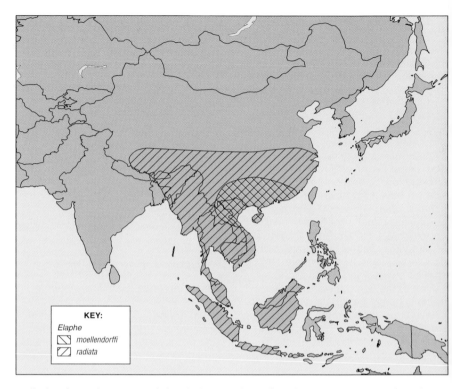

KEY:

Elaphe

◫ *moellendorffi*

◿ *radiata*

radiating from the eye, and the dark collar (with which the uppermost of the orbital stripes connects), are diagnostic of the species.

Both hypomelanistic (lacking much melanin) and anerythristic (lacking all red pigment) specimens of the radiated rat snake are known.

The Chinese King and the Steppes Rat Snakes

The Chinese King Rat Snake
(Elaphe carinata)

"Stinking Goddess" and "Chinese Stink Snake" are two names used by American dealers, for the variable but often very pretty, *E. carinata*. The names refer to *E. carinata*'s remarkably large musk glands and an extraordinary ability to produce scent if it chooses. But, in handling a fair num-

ber of *carinata,* we have not found them any more prone to "musk" than many other rat snake species. A third name for the species is "Chinese king rat snake." We don't know if this name relates to the regal size (a heavy-bodied 7 feet [2.1 m]) and haughty demeanor of the species or the kingsnake-like pattern and feeding habits of most examples.

Behavior: Like many of its Asian congeners, *E. carinata* can epitomize the word belligerence. The fact that they are long and of considerable girth, and also can inflate their bodies further when aggravated, certainly accentuates the impressiveness of their S-shaped striking pose. Although some captives will tame with time, others remain irascible.

Range and availability: The Chinese king rat snake ranges from

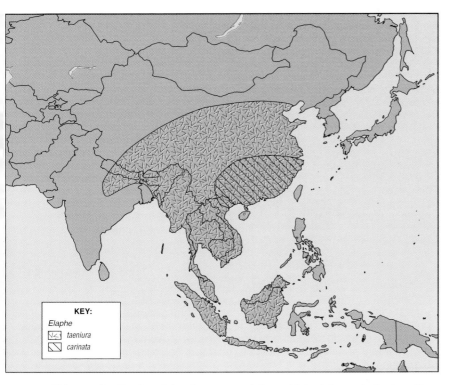

KEY:

Elaphe

taeniura

carinata

eastern China to the Ryukyu Islands. Its availability in the United States is sporadic, but when it is available, it is a fairly inexpensive species.

Coloration: Like many other rat snakes, the king rat undergoes marked ontogenetic changes and is naturally variable. Hatchling and juvenile specimens are quite dull, the ground color often being a pale olive-brown or an equally pale olive-green. Obscure to rather well-defined crossbands and/or variable spotting are usually present on juvenile specimens. The banding tends to be strongest anteriorly and the spotting most prevalent posteriorly. The ground color darkens with growth until some specimens become an inky black, while others merely become a darker olive. Those black specimens usually develop a brilliant yellow spot in the center of most scales while retaining a hint of the anterior banding. The edges of the scales and interstitial skin remains black. Snakes of this phase are remarkably beautiful. The olive-colored adults develop white and black interstitial skin anteriorly, retain light anterior banding, and, unless upset and inflated, appear rather unicolored posteriorly. Actually, the posterior interstitial skin is dark and shows best when the snake is in a defensive posture or distended with food.

Variation: This is yet another divergent Asian *Elaphe*. It varies both morphologically and in habits from its many congeners. Even the adults have a tendency to consume cold-blooded (ectothermic) prey items. Both snakes (including smaller examples of their own species) and lizards are eagerly consumed. Some specimens show a marked and irreversible preference for

Further research may determine that Elaphe carinata *is not truly a rat snake.*

ectotherms over the more traditional endotherms. Unlike most rat snakes, the vast majority of which have round pupils, at least some specimens of *E. carinata* have teardrop-shaped pupils. This divergent shape is most noticeable when the snakes are in bright light.

Breeding: If cycled with a normal period of brumation, *E. carinata* is not difficult to breed. The clutches can number more than a dozen large eggs and the hatchlings are of relatively large size at emergence. At a temperature of 81 to 85°F (27–29°C), incubation may vary from just over a month to just under two months. Although some hatchlings will accept rodent prey, many insist on lizards for their first few meals. Scenting a mouse with lizard feces or blood may induce an otherwise reluctant snake to accept the rodent.

The Steppes Rat Snake
(Elaphe dione)

Although not a favorite of American hobbyists, this rather gentle but dull rat snake is occasionally seen on dealers' lists. Although not a common species

in the United States, it is extensively bred by European herpetoculturists. The Steppes rat snake is much like a particularly dull, obscurely blotched, olive-brown, twin-spotted rat snake, *E. bimaculata*, in appearance. In fact, it appears to be quite closely allied to this latter species.

Range: The range of the Steppes rat snake extends over most of central Asia. It may be encountered from near sea level to rather high elevations, and is rather generally recognized as an important predator of rodents.

Brumation: The Steppes rat snake requires a lengthy period of hibernation to induce reproductive cycling. A *minimum* of 90 days is suggested and some breeders have suggested that between 120 and 150 days is more satisfactory.

Incubation: In keeping with many northern latitude rat snakes, the incubation duration of *E. dione* is greatly reduced from that of species from more southerly climes. Normal incubation usually varies from two to three weeks at 82°F (28°C).

Diet: Although we have never bred this species, we have been told that hatchlings readily accept pinky mice as their first meal.

Size: Adults of this interesting little snake range from 30 to about 36 inches (76–91 cm) in total length.

A Japanese Rat Snake

This is a nervous snake that is much more popular with Asian and European hobbyists than with American herpetoculturists. In fact, neither the normal (the Aodaisho) nor the albino (Shirohebi) morphs of this hardy, quiet snake are often found in the American market. Although dealers may call it *the* Japanese rat snake, it is by no means the only Japanese rat snake—so we'll use the specific native names for the normal and albino forms.

Two color morphs: In its normal coloration, the Aodaishu is anything but colorful. The ground color can vary from the dullest of olive-gray to a reasonably bright olive-yellow-green. The most consistent single marking is a dark postorbital bar that extends downward from the eye to the angle of the mouth. Some adults are vaguely saddled; some bear four vague lines; others (especially young adults) combine the two. The pair of dorsolateral stripes tend to be better defined than the lateral stripes. Indeed, in some phases, only two dorsolateral stripes are visible. Hatchlings and juveniles are very like the adults, but with slightly better-defined patterns.

The albino phase—the Shirohebi—is rigidly protected. It occurs in the wild in fair numbers, in the vicinity of the city of Iwakuni. Hatchlings bear traces of saddles; adult snakes are red-eyed and a unicolored pinkish-white. Even wild specimens show signs of protracted inbreeding. Inbred specimens demonstrate abnormalities in scalation as well as abnormally large eyes.

E. climacophora seems both well known and tolerated in its native Japan. It is said to be relatively common, even near human habitations, and is recognized immediately as an important predator of mice and rats. Besides rodents, this species accepts birds and their eggs.

Size and breeding: Adults may measure 5 feet (1.5 m). Females seem to mature somewhat more slowly than the males. Even heavily fed captive specimens on which the growth is "pushed" seldom become sexually active until their third year of life, and it is more often during their fourth or fifth year that sexual maturity is reached.

Reproduction: The smaller and younger females produce fewer, smaller, and seemingly less viable eggs than older, larger females. Clutches can number from three to 18 eggs, with between 10 and 13 seemingly being the norm. Like many Asiatic rat snakes, the eggs of this species seem to incubate more successfully at rather cool temperatures. We have had eggs successfully hatch after 65 days at 76°F (24°C). Total mortality of partially developed embryos occurred in a clutch that inadvertently reached 87°F (30°C). Whether mortality was caused by the warmth (this temperature can be tolerated by the eggs of many other rat snake species) or was merely coincidental is unknown.

Cycling: A winter brumation of about 90 days does much to cycle this species to reproductive activity. As with most other rat snakes, multiple clutches are possible (double-clutching is less well documented in the more northerly of any Old World species). In fact, a single clutch a season is an achievement.

Captive care: Our *E. climacophora* were housed in a fairly large and tall cage. They quickly found and extensively used as their hiding spots some cockatiel nesting boxes that were

The Japanese E. climacophora *is not eagerly sought by American hobbyists. Adults are straw-yellow or olive with very obscure markings.*

affixed near the top of the cage. Although they were entirely capable of overpowering live rats of moderate size, the snakes much preferred prekilled meals.

The Common Trinket Rat Snake

This is another of the Asiatic *Elaphe* popular in Europe but seldom seen in the United States. European hobbyists have such an avid interest that export specimens are seldom available.

Coloration: Like many other *Elaphe*, the common trinket rat snake (or merely trinket snake, as it is referred to by European hobbyists), *E. helena,* is variably hued. While the darker specimens may not be awfully pretty, those on the lighter end of the spectrum (buff to yellow) are quite beautiful. At first glance, the coloration of these is reminiscent of a blonde phase Trans-Pecos rat snake, *Bogertophis s. subocularis* (see page 60).

The head of the trinket rat snake is usually patternless except for a dark suture between the two parietal scales and a dark (and variably discernible) postocular stripe. A pair of elongate dark nape stripes are almost invariably present, and are echoed with a second, ventrolateral pair.

The body pattern, more difficult to describe, must necessarily be divided into an anterior and posterior category. Anteriorly (but posterior to the neck stripes), the trinket rat snake bears irregularly edged, dark dorsal blotches. Dorsolaterally in these dark blotches are thin, even darker vestiges of striping. Laterally, the dark blotches often contain irregular light scales that, together, form a small light blotch. Posteriorly, the blotches become obscure and the dorsum often lightens; however, the flanks darken in an evenly but obscurely edged, broad lateral stripe. The venter is light and, if marked at all, is only lightly and irregularly clouded.

Size: This is a small to medium-sized rat snake with a proportionately slender body. The adult length averages 3 to 4 feet (0.9–1.2 m), sometimes reaching 5 feet (1.5 m). Males are slightly smaller than females.

Range: *E. helena* ranges over most of the Indian subcontinent, eastward to Nepal, and southward to Sri Lanka.

Breeding: Because of its basically tropical distribution, brumation is not needed for breeding. A simple cooling period is all that is needed to assure success in most cases, and successful breedings of this species abound with no winter cooling at all. Like many tropical rat snakes, *E. helena* will multiple-clutch in the course of each season. Needless to say, only those in very good condition should undergo multiple-clutching. Clutches typically number from four to seven eggs and, at 82–86°F (28–30°C), a normal incubation period is about 60 days.

Diet: The very few hatchlings that we have had have readily fed on newly born mice.

Behavior: Although newly collected wild specimens will readily bite, once acclimated, this is a quiet and easily

Not all specimens of the common trinket rat snake are as brightly colored as this example. Photographed at Glades Herp.

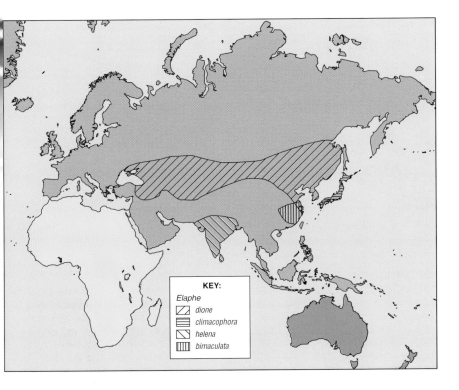

KEY:

Elaphe

▨	*dione*
▤	*climacophora*
◩	*helena*
⦀	*bimaculata*

handled rat snake. It is easy to see why breeders who work with the trinket rat snake become so enamored of it.

Two Lookalike Chinese Rat Snake Species

This is a short but difficult account about two pretty little Asian snakes. The first of these, the Chinese twin-spotted rat snake, *E. bimaculata*, presents no problem at all. It is a very typical, interesting little Asian rat snake that most hobbyists even consider a fairly hardy captive.

E. rufodorsata is more difficult, for, although it has long resided in the genus *Elaphe*, its placement therein is questionable at best. Unlike most of its congenors, this is a fish and frog eater. It has a stubby little snout and a low scale row count. All in all, the species looks more like a natricine (water

snakes and relatives) species than a rat snake.

E. bimaculata

Range and description: This little (28- to 36-inch [71–91 cm]) rat snake is more commonly seen in European collections than in America. It is tan, light brown, or buff with two rows of dark-edged spots of brownish-red to strawberry.

In one of its two rather distinctly different phases, this snake could be better called a four-striped rat snake. In this morph, the two rows of dorsal spots are joined into even-edged stripes by longitudinal extensions, and two lateral stripes are also prominent. There seems a tendency for this striped phase to be of an overall darker color than the more typical twin-spotted morph.

Twin-spotted rat snakes (E. bimaculata, *left) may be easily confused with* E. rufodorsata *(right). Both photographed at Gulf Coast Reptiles.*

The twin-spotted phase of *E. bimaculata* is quite attractive. The dorsolateral spots are often discrete anteriorly but may be joined posteriorly. There is a stylized spearpoint on the crown, the ends of which extend backward onto the neck as short stripes. Dark postorbital stripes begin at the angle of the mouth, pass diagonally upwards through each eye where they narrow, and continue as a dark (sometimes interrupted) line around the tip of the snout. Another marking, which passes over the top of the snout, connects the eyes. Lateral spots may be bold or poorly defined and may be discrete or joined, forming an irregular stripe.

Hibernation: As might be expected of a northern latitude rat snake, a period of winter dormancy will stimulate reproductive cycling. A three-month period of hibernation is suggested. Hibernation temperatures as low as 49°F (10°C) and as high as 59°F (16°C) have proven successful. Copulation may occur prior to, or following hibernation.

Breeding: Autumn breedings have resulted in fertile eggs being deposited the following spring with no other breedings occurring. Clutches are small (three to eight eggs) and eggs are large. The incubation duration is short, varying from three to four weeks. Hatchlings are 9 to 11 inches (22.8–27.9 cm) long and are duller but otherwise quite similar to their parents.

Diet: Newly born mice seem well accepted as a first meal.

E. rufodorsata

And, now on to the problematic *E. rufodorsata*, the definitely not-a-rat-snake, rat snake.

Description: In pattern and coloration *E. rufodorsata* is quite easily confused with *E. bimaculata*. The crown of the head bears an intricate, dark, anteriorly directed spearpoint. A dark chevron (either entire or interrupted at the point), again anteriorly directed, connects the eyes. The dorsal and lateral patterns are complex. In most cases, a well-defined, black-edged light (often buff) vertebral line runs from nape to tailtip. To both sides of this, anteriorly and medially, is a row of discrete, elongate, partial ocelli (see Glossary, page 100). Outlined with dark on the top and sides, the bottom

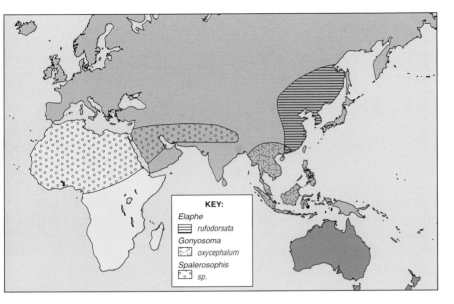

KEY:
Elaphe
≣ *rufodorsata*
Gonyosoma
⬡ *oxycephalum*
Spalerosophis
▱ *sp.*

of each ocellus is open and in contact with a light lateral line. Anteriorly, there are also two rows of irregular dark blotches on each side, one laterally, the second ventrolaterally. Posteriorly, the blotches fade and the overall appearance is of a striped snake. The belly is marked with irregular dark blotches and smudges. The dorsal ground color varies from tan to rufous.

Habits: The few *E. rufodorsata* that we have kept have quickly settled in and done reasonably well. We have found them to host numbers of endoparasites that can, if not purged, be debilitating over time.

We learned of their preference for fish and amphibian prey entirely by accident. The first specimens we had were unannounced and we had no place ready to house them. The group of four specimens—two males and two females—were placed, unceremoniously, in a tank with a pair of red-headed garter snakes, *Amphiesma stolata*. It was a large tank and the garters were small snakes that were, themselves, still in quarantine. A dozen

or so small fish—food for the garter snakes—swam in the water receptacle. Within minutes, the *E. rufodorsata* had found the water bowl and had eaten every last fish. Additional fish were eaten as readily. Newly metamorphosed Cuban tree frogs, *Osteopilus septentrionalis*, were also relished by the snakes. One small female *E. rufodorsata*, obviously gravid when received, gave birth to six small young that measured about 4.5 inches (11.4 cm) in total length. These readily ate small gambusia (live-bearing topminnows).

Gave birth? Yes, indeed! This is just another way in which this species diverges from the norm for the genus. Of the world's rat snakes, *E. rufodorsata* is the only ovoviviparous (live-bearing) species.

This species is seldom ordered purposely by either dealers or hobbyists. Those specimens that enter the pet trade in the United States are usually received in error (from the Chinese dealers who ship them as *E. bimaculata*).

Species Accounts: The Not-Really-Rat-Snake Rat Snakes

The Asian Genera *Gonyosoma* and *Spalerosophis*

If, to qualify for the name of rat snake, a snake need only *eat* rats, then the members of these two Old World genera are as much a rat snake as any other. However, if, to qualify for the title, a snake needs to be a close relative of *Elaphe*, the wisdom of referring to these species as rat snakes is more doubtful.

Gonyosoma oxycephalum

This red-tailed green rat snake was long a member of the genus *Elaphe*. Despite the fact that it has been imported to both the United States and Europe in some numbers for the last two decades, precious little is truly known about this snake. We do know that it has an immense distribution and is of very variable coloration.

Coloration: Typically, specimens from tropical Southeast Asia are usually of some shade of green (often leaf) with a tail of orange or red. The red coloration is brightest in the center of each scale, the sutures being paler red to gray. The supralabial (upper lip) scales are usually much brighter than the dorsal surface of the head. A dark eye stripe separates the two colors. The ventral coloration is usually paler (more yellowish) than the green of the dorsal and lateral scales.

Specimens from Java may be pearl gray, without a contrastingly colored tail, and have a mottled yellow to mottled green and yellow or solid gray head. The dorsal and lateral scales are darkest on the trailing edge, often having an interesting and beautiful scalloped look.

From other areas of the range, such as Celebes and surrounding islands, the ground color may be a warm tan, buff, or olive-brown. The tail may be gray to black or lack contrasting colors. The head is often at least tinged with yellow or pale green. In all cases, the lower sides and venter are at least somewhat lighter and a dark eye stripe is present.

Some color phases are afforded the subspecific names of *floweri* (a brown phase) or *jansenii* (a brown snake with dark flank stripes, supposedly restricted to the Celebes Islands). Given the immense variation of coloration seen in this snake within a specific range, these names would seem to be of questionable validity.

Captivity: Sadly, *Gonyosoma* are among the most difficult snakes to acclimate and therefore are poor captivity candidates. Most are very heavily parasitized or have advanced respiratory problems when imported. The debilitating problems of many are already irreversible when landed here. On the rare occasions when reasonably healthy red-tails are received, by immediately purging them of their parasite load, some may be saved.

Because wild collected specimens are so difficult to acclimate, the very few captive-bred red-tailed rat snakes that become available are expensive. In 1995, wild-caught adults sold for between $35 and $75 each, while captive-bred babies sold for $200 each.

Hatchlings: Most of the hatchlings currently offered are from incubated eggs laid by imported gravid females. Reported clutches are small, numbering from three to nine rather large, elongate eggs. The slender babies are from 15 to 19 inches (38–48 cm) in length at emergence. The hatchlings are similar to, but duller than the adults, especially prior to their postnatal shed. Although wild hatchlings reportedly feed on lizards and frogs, those that are captive-hatched seem not at all reluctant to accept suitably small mice.

Behavior: *G. oxycephalum* seems to be a highly arboreal species. Certainly, if given a spacious cage with sufficient height and branches on which to climb, these snakes will do so avidly and agilely. They will often loosely coil atop the highest branch to which they have access, surely an act of a species at home in the trees. To lend more support to this theory of extensive aboreality, when wild-caught specimens can be induced to feed, it is usually a bird that first tempts them.

Wild specimens have been reported from various arboreal positions, in trees and shrubs, often quite close to the water. In some areas *G. oxycephalum* is considered a mangrove snake and is closely associated with brackish and salt water.

In both appearance and demeanor, *Gonyosoma oxycephalum* is more racer-like than rat snake-like. Long (often to 8.5 feet [2.58 m], occasionally longer), slender snakes with narrow, but distinct, heads, and proportionately long noses, they are fast, alert, and very defensive. Many wild-collected speci-

Seen here are two color phases of the red-tailed green rat snake.

mens (and virtually all *are* wild-collected) steadfastly and vigorously resist handling. A large, vertically oriented cage in a quiet, low traffic area seems mandatory for this species. Stress-free management is also important. Provide this species with secure hiding areas in the form of bird nesting boxes affixed near the top of their cage.

Temperature: This is a low altitude tropical snake and as such prefers warm temperatures and high humidity. Low cage humidity will often result in shedding problems. The very few that we have successfully kept for varying

91

periods of time were at night temperatures of 75°F (24°C) and day temps of 88°F (31°C). Photoperiod was natural.

We consider green-tailed red rat snakes a species suitable for only the most advanced hobbyists or zoological institutions.

Spalerosophis

This is a species complex of "not-a-rat-snake rat snakes." If there is but a single species, there are about eight subspecies. The actual taxonomic arrangement varies according to the authority quoted. Because the most popular member of the genus, *S. diadema*, is referred to as the diadem rat snake, this name has been carried over to other forms as well. They are becoming so popular, and are referred to so often as rat snakes, that they are included in this book.

The members of the genus *Spalerosophis* are quite probably rather closely allied to the racers. They are diurnally active, aridland snakes of the Mideast, northern Africa, and central Asia, where, during the summer, very hot daytime temperatures are the norm.

Although usually referred to as rat snakes, the snakes of the genus Spalerosophis *may actually be more closely allied to the racers. This* S. diadema atriceps *was photographed at Glades Herp.*

Diadem rat snakes tend to be defensive bluffers, inflating their body, hissing, and feinting at approaching hands. Some bite; most don't. Even the large wild-collected adults that the author once imported became reasonably tractable with time.

Coloration: Most of these snakes have sandy to rich buff ground colors with large to small, darker saddles or blotches. There is a tendency for the neck markings to elongate to broken stripes (especially dorsolaterally) or attenuate blotches. The heads of some bear intricate patterns (the diadem markings from which the name is derived), while the heads of other specimens are so dark that patterns are all but obscured.

Feeding habits: The various diadem rat snakes are "search-and-overpower" hunters like the racers, rather than "wait-and-ambush" hunters like *Elaphe*. Although *Spalerosophis* can constrict, they are less efficient at this than the true rat snakes. As often as not, the various diadem rat snakes will grasp a prey item, then immobilize it by throwing a single loop of their body over the creature. Diadem rat snakes have powerful jaws and the bite of a large specimen can rather quickly suffocate a small rodent.

Captive care: If kept dry and warm, diadem rat snakes are hardy captives. Daytime temperatures of from 84 to 90°F (28–33°C) seem adequate. One end of the terrarium can be heated slightly by using an under-tank heating device. Nighttime temperatures can be allowed to drop by several degrees.

Reproduction: While a simple winter cooling and reduced photoperiod may cycle specimens from the southernmost reaches of the range for reproduction, more northerly specimens may require an actual period of hibernation. Since it is usually impossible to determine the origin of a given specimen once it has entered the pet trade, those who wish to breed diadem rat snakes opt for the period of full hibernation.

Male diadem rat snakes often attain sexual maturity at an earlier age than females. Males are capable of breeding at two to three years of age, females a year later.

Large females produce from 4 to 10 large eggs. The hatchlings are from 16 to 18 inches (40.6–45.7 cm) in length at hatching and are similar to the adults in pattern but of duller colors.

The subspecies: The most impressively colored of these snakes is the form known as the royal diadem rat snake, *S. diadema atriceps*. The distinct saddles of the juveniles fade and are replaced in maturity by irregular dark flecks and blotches. With maturity the sand-colored ground hue becomes buff to nearly terra-cotta. The diadem pattern on the head of the juveniles is obscured by increasing amounts of black and/or red. All in all, this 5.5-foot-long (1.67 m) desert-dweller is impressive and well worth keeping. Although some specimens may display impressively, most quiet quickly. This subspecies is now bred in fair numbers by both American and European hobbyists. The royal diadem rat snake ranges widely in suitable habitats in India, Pakistan, and surrounding countries.

The Egyptian diadem rat snake, *S. diadema cliffordi*, is a paler and less prettily colored race. Although the pattern of the juveniles may fade some with advancing age, this form retains prominent markings throughout its lifetime.

The blotched diadem rat snake, *S. (diadema) arenarius*, is also a beautiful species. The ground color of this Pakistani snake is often a pale sandy-tan, and the numerous but rather small middorsal blotches (and even smaller lateral blotches) may vary from warm brown to almost a strawberry red. This species also attains a length of more than 5 feet (1.5 m). Although once rather common in the American pet trade, the blotched diadem rat snake is now rarely seen.

The Tropical American *Spilotes* and *Pseustes*

The neotropical snakes of the genera *Spilotes* and *Pseustes* are slender, attenuate arborealists that are occasionally sold as tropical rat snakes or as tropical chicken snakes. These are pretty, often bad-tempered, fairly slender snakes. Even healthy, long-term captive specimens of both genera have a malnourished, keeled-back appearance. They are usually rather heavily parasitized when imported. Neither is captive-bred in large numbers.

These snakes are included here simply because they are sold as rat snakes and few of their buyers are aware of the inaccurate identification.

Behavior: When frightened, the snakes of both genera inflate their throats (vertically), draw back into a loose striking "S," and defend themselves through repeated strikes. If contact is made with the offending object, they are not at all hesitant to follow through with slashing bites. Both

KEY:
Pseustes sp.
Spilotes sp.

Tropical rat snakes of the genus Spilotes *can vary from all yellow to all black. Like most specimens, this example is intermediate. Photographed at Gulf Coast Reptiles.*

monly seen in the pet market. The several species of *Pseustes* are of quite similar appearance, differing mainly in the numbers of keeled or unkeeled scale rows (this can be hard to determine on an angry, biting snake). *P. sulphureus* has all dorsal and lateral scales keeled except for the row directly above the widened ventral scutes. *P. poecilonotus* usually has the lowest several rows of lateral scales unkeeled. *Pseustes* are, for the most part, big olive-green to sulphur-yellow snakes (with or without dorsal striping).

The following comments pertain equally to the snakes of the two genera.

Behavior: The neotropical rat snakes can be quite hardy as captives. They are agile and active climbers that, apparently, normally range over a quite extensive home territory. Two *Pseustes sulphureus* seen in Amazonian Peru were moving along the ridgepole of a thatch-roofed tourist complex. A pair, the large (8 foot [2.4 m]) male seemed to be trailing the smaller (6.5 foot[1.98 m]) female along her (artificial) arboreal highway, some 20 feet (6 m) above the ground. It was apparent that the pair had come in from the surrounding forest only that morning, for the area, ridgepole included, had been searched for snakes late the evening before. How deep in the forest the snakes actually originated is unknown. The preference of *Spilotes* for arboreal travel was demonstrated by a specimen in Yucatan. Although on the ground when first spotted, the snake turned and darted into some thornscrub, ascended a vine, and continued its exit across the tops of the low (15 feet [4.56 m]) thornbrush. The specimen would have actually been better concealed had it remained on the ground.

Caging and temperature: The above discourse was simply a long way of saying that the tropical rat

Spilotes and Pseustes can near 10 feet (3 m) in length and their bites can be unforgettable.

The snakes of these two genera are of quite different color, with *Spilotes pullatus*, the tropical rat snake (actually a principally arboreal snake species more closely allied with the racers) being the prettiest.

Range and coloration: *S. pullatus* ranges in one of five subspecies from tropical Mexico through South America to northern Mexico. Most specimens are black snakes that are variably banded or speckled with yellow. In some cases, the coloration is reversed and we have a primarily *yellow* snake with black bands or speckles. Occasionally, solid black specimens, and, even more rarely, solid yellow specimens, are encountered. In our opinion, it is the yellow specimens with variable black bands that are the prettiest.

Appearance: Of the usually bad-tempered *Pseustes*, only two, *sulphureus* (a species of equatorial Latin America), and *poecilonotus* (which ranges from Oaxaca, Mexico southward to the Amazon Basin) are com-

snakes prefer to be above the ground. They should be provided with sizable, vertically oriented cages that are equipped with numerous horizontal limbs. Do keep in mind that the members of both genera are active by nature and can attain a full 9+ feet (2.7 m) in total length. High temperatures (80–90°F, [27-33°C]), high relative humidity, and ample fresh drinking water should be provided. Nighttime temperatures can be allowed to drop by a few degrees.

Feeding habits: Neither of these snakes are constrictors. They grasp their prey in their strong jaws and immobilize it by throwing a loop of their body over it. That this is not always an effective way of subduing rodents is displayed by the anterior scars borne by many *Pseustes* and *Spilotes* seen in the wild. Opportunistic feeders, these snakes eat, besides rodents, birds, amphibians, and other reptiles.

Although both genera of the tropical rat snakes have long been available in the pet trade, they seem to be finding favor with hobbyists only now. Understandably, of the two, *Spilotes* is the favorite. Although *Spilotes* has proven a problematic breeder, a few

Because of the confusingly variable common names, it is best to refer to snakes of the genus Pseustes *by their scientific names. This is* P. sulphureus. *Note the inflated throat and lolling tongue.*

successes have been recorded by both private hobbyists and zoological gardens. Clutches recorded have been rather small in egg number, most ranging from 6 to 17 eggs. The hatchlings are long (16 to 20 inches [40.6–50.8 cm]) and slender, and feed readily on small mice. Hatchlings are mini-replicas of the adults.

Photograph Them and Leave Them Behind!

Photographing rat snakes can be a demanding but fulfilling pursuit. Many hobbyists see photography as the best way to document both captive and wild behavior patterns. It is a pursuit that we enjoy immensely. It gives us an excuse for getting into the field and/or it is a way of "keeping" a rat snake with no work—once the photograph has been taken and developed. Taking successful photographs of rat snakes can truly exercise your patience. Even the tamest among them often prefer to continue to move—ever so slowly—but certainly enough to cause image blurring on the film. Photographing a specimen in the field can be even more difficult. Photography requires that stealth and field knowledge be combined with a knowledge of your camera and its accessories. We carry a backup camera body, lenses of various sizes, 10 or 12 rolls of film, and a portable stage in the back of our car. At some time or other we not only use all of this gear but wish we had more! As you progress, each photo will help you to see how the next could be improved. Getting started is easy.

Equipment

The equipment required will depend upon a number of variables. Among these are whether you will be indulging in both long-distance field photos and staged closeups. Of course, photographing captive or staged rat snakes is often easier than pursuing and photographing free-ranging ones, but not nearly as satisfying.

Some Photographic Hints

• For staged photography, create a small natural setting by placing rocks, mosses, leaves, or bark—whichever is most appropriate for the species you're photographing—on a stage. We use a small lazy Susan as a stage. This enables us to rotate the stage with the animal on it, for different photographic angles. This works, providing that you move *very slowly*, both in your own actions and in rotating the stage. If you don't have a lazy Susan, just arrange the setting items on a tabletop or on a tree stump (outdoors or in, depending on where you are at the time), put the rat snake in place (it may take quite a while to quiet it!), focus, and shoot.

A simple photography stage can be made from a plastic garbage can and a lazy Susan base.

Basic Equipment Needs

A sturdy 35 mm camera body with interchangeable lenses is suggested. You don't necessarily need a brand-new camera body and lenses—we've used quality second-hand equipment for many of my photographic ventures. You *do* need a photo supply dealer who can accurately advise you about the condition of the equipment you're buying, and who can tell you about some features of that particular lens or body (usually, second-hand camera equipment does not come with manuals of any sort).

A 35mm camera body can be fairly inexpensive if purchased second-hand.

Lenses: those we use include
- 28 mm wide angle for habitat photos
- 50 mm standard for habitat photos
- 105 mm macro for closeups (suitable for almost every purpose)
- 75–205 mm zoom lens for variable field work
- 400 mm fixed focal length telephoto lens for field work
- 120–600 zoom lens for distant but variable field work

Strobes: A series of dedicated strobes (a dedicated strobe inter-faces with the camera f-stop setting to furnish appropriate light levels).

Lens adapter: An ×1.25 power magnifier or an ×2 doubler.

Film: ISO 50 slide film is slower and less "grainy" than higher speed films. This slower film will give you the best results, but also requires a bright day or electronic flashes to compensate for the slow speed. The higher the ISO, the less light you will need to photograph, but the "grainier" your pictures will be. If you are taking pictures with the hopes of having them published, use ISO 50 slide film. If you are taking photos merely for your own enjoyment, use either slide or print film, as you prefer.

Tripod: A sturdy tripod (an absolute necessity for the telephoto lenses) will hold your camera steady while you squeeze off that "once in a lifetime" shot. Camera equipment with lenses is heavy, especially if you're out in the field and have slogged through hip-deep water then scaled a couple of hillsides. The equipment is heavy even if you're indoors.

Camera body: After having a camera body malfunction on occasion, we now always have at least one spare body available.

A variety of lenses will enable you to focus on different fields.

Use a tripod to avoid blurred shots.

Having a photo assistant to help pose or catch the snake will help.

• We used the top half of a round trash or garbage can for the backing of our stage. We first cut it to size, than firmly bolted it in place. Black velvet clipped into place around the inside surface of the background gives a good background. The result is an easily moved, eminently serviceable stage.

• If you're trying field photography, approach the animal slowly and obliquely. Avoid eye contact. If the snake notices you (as it almost certainly will) freeze for a moment, then begin moving again. Eventually, if you are lucky, you will be close enough to make the field shot for which you were hoping.

• When finished, retrace your steps carefully, disturbing as little habitat as possible, and leaving nothing behind—nothing, that is, except your footprints and the specimen you just successfully photographed.

Glossary

aestivation: period of warm weather inactivity, often triggered by excessive heat or drought.

aglyphous: having solid teeth.

albino: lacking normal black pigment.

allopatric: not occurring together, but often adjacent.

ambient temperature: temperature of the surrounding environment.

anal plate: large scute (or scutes) covering the snake's anus.

anerythristic: lacking red pigment.

anterior: toward the front.

anus: external opening of the cloaca; the vent.

arboreal: tree-dwelling.

brille: transparent "spectacle" covering the eyes of a snake.

brumation: reptilian and amphibian equivalent of mammalian hibernation.

caudal: pertaining to the tail.

cb/cb: captive-bred, captive-born.

cb/ch: captive-bred, captive-hatched.

chorioallantois: gas-permeable membranous layer inside the shell of a reptile egg.

cloaca: common chamber into which digestive, urinary, and reproductive systems empty, and which itself opens exteriorly through the vent or anus.

constricting: to wrap tightly in coils and squeeze.

convergent evolution: evolution of two unrelated species as the result of environmental conditions.

crepuscular: active at dusk and/or dawn.

deposition: as used here, the laying of the eggs or birthing of young.

deposition site: spot chosen by the female to lay her eggs or have young.

dimorphic: difference in form, build, or coloration involving the same species; often sex-linked.

diurnal: active in the daytime.

dorsal: pertaining to the back; upper surface.

dorsolateral: pertaining to the upper sides.

dorsum: upper surface.

ecological niche: precise habitat utilized by a species.

ectothermic: cold-blooded.

endemic: confined to a specific region.

endothermic: warm-blooded.

erythristic: prevalence of red pigment.

form: identifiable species or subspecies.

fossorial: adapted for burrowing; a burrowing species.

genus: taxonomic classification of a group of species having similar characteristics. The genus falls between the next higher designation of "family" and the next lower designation of "species." Genera is the singular of genus. It is always capitalized when written.

glottis: opening of the windpipe.

gravid: reptilian equivalent of mammalian pregnancy.

gular: pertaining to the throat.

heliothermic: pertaining to a species that basks in the sun to thermoregulate.

hemipenes: dual copulatory organs of male lizards and snakes.

hemipenis: singular form of hemipenes.

herpetoculture: captive breeding of reptiles and amphibians.

herpetoculturist: one who indulges in herpetoculture.

herpetologist: one who indulges in herpetology.

herpetology: study (often scientifically oriented) of reptiles and amphibians.

hibernacula: winter dens.

hybrid: offspring resulting from the breeding of two species.

hydrate: to restore body moisture by drinking or absorption.

insular: as used here, island-dwelling.

intergrade: offspring resulting from the breeding of two subspecies, often occuring naturally in the wild.

Jacobson's organs: highly enervated olfactory pits in the palate of snakes and lizards.

juvenile: a young or immature specimen.

keel: a ridge (along the center of a scale).

labial: pertaining to the lips.

lateral: pertaining to the side.

leucistic: different than albinism, leucism is caused by defects in all chromatophores. Leucistic animals are often pure white and lack a pattern. The eyes of most examples are blue or black.

melanism: a profusion of black pigment.

mental: the scale at the tip of the lower lip.

middorsal: pertaining to the middle of the back.

midventral: pertaining to the center of the belly or abdomen.

monotypic: containing but one type.

nocturnal: active at night.

ocellus (*pl* ocelli): a spot of color (eyespot) encircled by another color.

ontogenetic: age-related (color and/or pattern) changes.

oviparous: reproducing by means of eggs that hatch after laying.

ovoviviparous: reproducing by means of shelled or membrane-contained eggs that hatch prior to, or at deposition.

photoperiod: daily/seasonally variable length of the hours of daylight.

poikilothermic: a species with no internal body temperature regulation; the old term was "cold-blooded."

postocular: to the rear of the eye.

prehensile: adapted for grasping.

premaxillary: bones at the front of the upper jaw.

prey imprinting: preferring prey of only a particular species and/or color.

race: a subspecies.

rostral: the (often modified) scale on the tip of the snout.

scute: scale.

species: a group of similar creatures that produce viable young when breeding. The taxonomic designation that falls beneath genus and above subspecies; abbreviation: "sp."

subspecies: subdivision of a species. A race that may differ slightly in color, size, scalation, or other criteria; abbreviation: "ssp."

sympatric: occurring together.

taxonomy: science of classification of plants and animals.

terrestrial: land-dwelling.

thermoreceptive: sensitive to heat.

thermoregulate: to regulate (body) temperature by choosing a warmer or cooler environment.

vent: external opening of the cloaca; the anus.

venter: underside of a creature; the belly.

ventral: pertaining to the undersurface or belly.

ventrolateral: pertaining to the sides of the venter (belly).

Useful Addresses and Literature

Amateur Societies

Despite the fact that corn and rat snakes are among the most popular of reptiles, there are no clubs or societies dedicated to them alone. However, among the members of most herpetological societies, there are usually many who are interested in these snakes.

You may also learn of the existence of regional herpetological societies by asking biology teachers/professors, curators or other workers at museums and nature centers, or at pet stores.

Northern Ohio Association of
   Herpetologists (NOAH)
Dept. of Biology
Case Western Reserve University
Cleveland, OH 44106

Chicago Herpetological Society
   2001 N. Clark St.
Chicago, IL 60614

Gainesville Herpetological Society
P.O. Box 140353
Gainesville, FL 32614-0353

Central Florida Herpetological Society
P.O. Box 3277
Winter Haven, FL 33881

Northern California Herpetological
   Society
Box 1363
Davis, CA 95617-1363

Professional Herpetological Societies

Herpetologist's League
   c/o Texas Natural Heritage Program
Texas Parks and Wildlife Dept.
4200 Smith School Rd.
Austin, TX 78744

Society for the Study of Amphibians
   and Reptiles
Dept. of Zoology
Miami University
Oxford, OH 45056

Magazines

Reptiles Magazine
P.O. Box 6050
Mission Viejo, CA 92690

Reptile and Amphibian Magazine
RD3, Box 3709-A
Pottsville, PA 17901

Reptilian Magazine
22 Firs Close
Hazlemere, High Wycombe
Bucks HP15 7TF, England

Books and Articles

Arnold, E.N. and J. A. Burton. *A Field Guide to the Reptiles and Amphibians of Britain and Europe*. London: Collins, 1978.

Bartlett, Richard D. *In Search of Reptiles and Amphibians*. Leiden: E.J. Brill, 1988.

_____. *Digest for the Successful Terrarium*. Morris Plains, NJ: TetraPress, 1989.

Bartz, H. and V. Scheidt. "Care and Breeding of the Chinese Twin-Spotted Rat Snake, *Elaphe bimaculata*." *The Vivarium*, 2(2):8–10, 1989.

Conant, Roger and Joseph T. Collins. *A Field Guide to Reptiles and Amphibians; Eastern and Central North America*. Boston: Houghton Mifflin, 1991.

Cranston, T. "Natural History and Captive Husbandry of the Western Green Rat Snake." *The Vivarium* 2(1):8–11, 29, 1989.

Dowling, Herndon G. A Taxonomic Study of the Rat Snakes, Genus *Elaphe fitzinger*. II. The subspecies of *Elaphe flavirufa* (Cope), Ann Arbor, MI: U of MI, 1952.

_____. A taxonomic study of the rat snakes, genus *Elaphe fitzinger*. V. The Rosaliae Section. Ann Arbor: U of MI, 1957.

_____. A taxonomic study of the rat snakes. VI. Validation of the genera *Gonyosoma wagler* and *Elaphe fitzinger*, Copeia (1):29–40, 1958.

_____. A taxonomic study of the rat snakes, genus *Elaphe fitzinger*. VII. The triaspis section. Zoologica 45: 53–80, 1960.

Mehrtens, John M. *Living Snakes of the World in Color*. New York: Sterling Publications, 1987.

Pope, Clifford H. *The Reptiles of China*. New York: American Museum of Natural History, 1935.

Stebbins, Robert C. *A Field Guide to Western Reptiles and Amphibians*. Boston: Houghton Mifflin, 1985.

Staszko, Ray and Jerry G. Walls. *Rat Snakes: A Hobbyist's Guide to Elaphe and Kin*. Neptune, NJ: TFH, 1994.

Wright, Albert H. and A. A. Wright. *Handbook of Snakes*. Vol. I. Ithaca, NY: Comstock, 1957.

Index

(**Bold** = photo)